MIA HAMM

GREAT AMERICANS IN SPORTS

MIA HAMM

MATT CHRISTOPHER

Little, Brown and Company

New York Boston

Little, Brown and Company

Hachette Book Group
1290 Avenue of the Americas, New York, NY 10104
Visit us at lb-kids.com

mattchristopher.com

Little, Brown and Company is a division of Hachette Book Group, Inc.
The Little, Brown name and logo are trademarks of Hachette Book Group, Inc.

The publisher is not responsible for websites (or their content) that are not owned by the publisher.

First Great Americans in Sports Edition: September 2015
Originally published as *On the Field with...Mia Hamm* in September 1998 by Little, Brown and Company

Text revised and updated by Zachary Rau
Cover illustration by Michael Cho

Matt Christopher® is a registered trademark of Matt Christopher Royalties, Inc.

Library of Congress Cataloging-in-Publication Data

Christopher, Matt, 1917–1997.
    [On the field with—Mia Hamm]
    Great Americans in sports, Mia Hamm / Matt Christopher. — First Great Americans in Sports Edition.
        pages cm
    "Originally published as On the field with—Mia Hamm in September 1998 by Little, Brown and Company"—T.p. verso.
    "Text revised and updated by Zachary Rau"—T.p. verso.
    Audience: Age: 8–12.
    ISBN 978-0-316-26101-2 (trade pbk.) — ISBN 978-0-316-26100-5 (ebook) — ISBN 978-0-316-26102-9 (library edition ebook)   1. Hamm, Mia, 1972—Juvenile literature.   2. Women soccer players—United States—Biography—Juvenile literature.   I. Title.
    GV942.7.H27C57 2015
    796.334092—dc23
    [B]

                                                                    2015011635

10 9 8 7 6 5 4 3 2

RRD-C

Printed in the United States of America

CONTENTS

INTRODUCTION

On the afternoon of August 1, 1996, more than seventy-six thousand spectators poured into Sanford Stadium on the campus of the University of Georgia in Athens, Georgia. There was nothing unusual about that. The university's football team, the Bulldogs, regularly packed the stadium with at least that many fans when they played their home games during football season.

The stadium wasn't packed with fans for a Georgia Bulldogs game or for any American football game, though. People from all over the world had come to Athens to watch a game of soccer. To be more specific, they had all come to see who would win the first gold-medal game in women's Olympic soccer, the United States or the People's Republic of China. Millions more across the world were watching on television as the superstar of women's soccer, Mia Hamm, led the United States against China's team. Never before had so many people gathered to watch a women's sporting event.

Only a few decades earlier, the idea that so many

1

people would watch a soccer game played by women would have been hard to believe. For most of the twentieth century, women were taken seriously in only a handful of sports. Track and field, golf, tennis, gymnastics, basketball, and figure skating were considered sports women could play without needing to be too physical. Many people thought sports like soccer were simply too rough for women to play. During those years, young women were constantly reminded of the notion that sports were for boys. Girls, on the other hand, were expected to engage in other activities—like homemaking, or standing on the sidelines and cheering on the boys. It wasn't until the introduction of Title IX, an amendment that outlawed gender discrimination at schools and colleges receiving money from the government, that women's athletics was finally given even a small portion of the attention it deserved.

Soccer, or what the rest of the world calls football, was the most popular sport in the world and started to become more popular in the United States as boys' and girls' youth leagues sprang up across the country during the late 1960s and early 1970s. But only a few women in the entire world played competitive professional-level soccer. Not many people even knew that women played soccer. In the United States, only a few high schools had a women's soccer team. It wasn't until 1978 that a college or university would field a varsity women's soccer program! There was no such thing as a national team or women's World Cup competition. No one thought that women would someday play soccer in the Olympics, let alone have their own professional leagues all over the world.

It was strong and talented women like Mia Hamm who changed all of that. Mia Hamm is without a doubt one of the greatest athletes of this century. Her playing and drive helped make the US women's national team one of the greatest in sports history. Mia caught the attention of the world with her play and became an ambassador for the sport. Her success has been hard-earned, and it all started when a toddler fell in love with soccer.

CHAPTER ONE
1972–1976

CHASING THE BALL

As the story goes, it was a warm day in 1973 when the toddler of the young Hamm family saw a boy and his father kicking a ball back and forth. No one in the family understood the game very well, but little Mia, the fourth of six Hamm children, loved what she saw. As she stood close to her parents, she never took her eyes off the black-and-white soccer ball. After a missed pass, she sprang after the ball and gave it one big whack. She had been born with a clubfoot, which required a corrective boot, and she was still learning to run and walk, but she managed to keep the ball from an older boy before giving the ball another mighty kick.

From that day forward, Mia dreamed of playing "the beautiful game," as soccer is often called. She didn't know that girls weren't "supposed to" play sports. For her, it was fun to chase after the ball and kick it, to run around with other children, then sit and play in the grass together, making friends.

That's how Mia Hamm's soccer career began. Years later, her love of the sport and the friendships she made on the field would take her all over the world and make her the most well-known female athlete of all time. But that was still a long ways off.

Mariel Margaret Hamm was born on March 17, 1972, in Selma, Alabama. Her father, William, was a pilot in the United States Air Force, and the family moved around a lot. Her mother, Stephanie, was a ballerina. Soon after she was born, her mother started calling her Mia because her daughter reminded her of one of her former ballet teachers, the world-famous ballerina Mia Slavenska.

As a member of the air force, Bill Hamm was never stationed in one place for very long. In 1973, he was transferred to Italy. The entire family, which then included Mia's older brother and two older sisters, moved to Florence, Italy.

When he wasn't flying airplanes, Bill Hamm loved to watch sports. But in Italy, hardly anyone played the sports Bill was used to watching in the United States. Bill liked baseball, football, and basketball. In Italy, the most popular sport was soccer, which was a huge part of the culture there. Men, women, and children all loved the sport. The stadiums on match days were always packed. The country would practically shut down when the national team played since everyone was focused on the game.

Wherever the family went, it seemed as if someone was playing soccer. In almost every open field or empty street, clusters of young boys raced after a soccer ball. Virtually every town had a men's team, and larger cities often supported several soccer clubs. Most teams were amateur, but the Italians also sponsored several thriving professional leagues. Thousands of fans turned out to support their favorite team, chanting and singing in unison in the stands while waving huge flags and banners. Televised soccer games were the most popular programs in the country.

When Bill started watching soccer, he didn't understand the game that well. Soccer wasn't very popular in the United States. Only a few public schools and colleges had soccer teams. The North American Soccer League was the professional league in America, but few people went to the games and they were rarely televised. Only a handful of the players were from the United States. Most were from Europe and South America. In the United States, Bill hadn't paid much attention to the game.

But in Italy, he had little choice. If he wanted to watch sports, he had to watch soccer. Luckily, soccer was everywhere. The more he watched, the more he began to appreciate the sport. He realized that what had first looked to him like a bunch of players randomly running after a ball was actually a sport that demanded great athletic skill and strategy. He learned that every player on the team played a specific position, just like in basketball or hockey, and each position had different responsibilities. The more Bill learned about the game, the more he grew to love it. It didn't take long for Italy to convert Bill into a rabid soccer supporter.

The family loved to do everything together, and Bill started taking his family to soccer games. The children, particularly Mia, took to the game immediately. She was small for her age and usually quite shy, but when she saw a soccer ball her eyes would light up. On the air force base, she often joined other children for pickup games of soccer.

When Bill was transferred to the United States a few years later, he and the Hamms brought soccer back with them. It had gotten under their skin. The only problem was that Bill and Stephanie would have to find soccer for their kids. Little League Baseball and other youth sports programs like Pop Warner football were commonplace in the United States, but youth soccer programs were still hard to find. When the Hamms finally landed in Wichita Falls, Texas, Stephanie and Bill were excited to find that youth soccer in Texas was as popular as football or baseball—or at least it was close.

Slowly but surely, soccer's popularity had risen in the States since the Hamms had moved to Italy. Brazilian soccer star Pelé, the best player to ever play the game, had signed with the New York Cosmos in 1975 and ignited an excitement for the sport in every major American city. The North American Soccer League (NASL) had gone from an afterthought to a real and viable league the moment Pelé signed with the Cosmos. His popularity and his play had started a soccer revolution in the United States. Teams had sprouted in Seattle, Los Angeles, Miami, Philadelphia, San Diego, and Portland, and even as far north as Vancouver, Canada. The NASL was growing at a phenomenal rate, and so was the popularity of the sport. Pelé's signing had opened the floodgates for soccer in America. Some of the best players from Europe began to pour into the US soccer market. European Footballer of the Year George Best; German World Cup winner Franz Beckenbauer; Bobby Moore, who captained England to the 1966 World Cup; three-time European Footballer of the Year Johan Cruyff; and Italian Giorgio Chinaglia all took a chance on the NASL in America. With the influx of talent, the games got more technical and more strategic, and the quality of the games improved dramatically. Americans were exposed to a level of soccer that had previously been seen only in Europe and South America—and they loved it.

The excitement of watching Pelé and the other great footballers of that era play the game as it was meant to be played had infected the country. Wanting to be just like their heroes, thousands of kids started joining youth leagues, and new leagues popped up in cities from coast to coast. Even after Pelé left the Cosmos and soccer's popularity dipped again in the United States, kids still had fun playing soccer, and adults were happy to organize teams and leagues. The game was so simple, and the fact that it didn't require a lot of equipment made it easy to start a new league in any state, and in most seasons. All it took was a grassy field and a ball, and players could learn the game. And anyone who could kick a ball or defend a goal could play. For parents, one of the best things about soccer was that every player got to touch the ball. Everyone was included.

Because soccer is a sport that relies more on speed and agility than strength and size, it is one of the few sports boys and girls can play together. Kids of similar ages, both male and female, are able to compete equally.

When Mia's older sisters and brother found out there was a league in town, they wanted to play. Bill was delighted and did his best to support his children. He was still learning the finer points of the game, so he started studying the rules and fundamentals of youth soccer. He became a coach and referee so that he could learn even more and make sure his children learned how to play correctly. He studied every book about soccer he could find.

At first, Mia wasn't allowed to play on a team. She was just too young. Yet the family spent most of every Saturday at the soccer field. Mia loved watching her siblings and the other kids play. Every time an errant kick came her way, she was off and running after it. Her mother often spent her Saturdays chasing after Mia!

Mia's mother recognized that her daughter was full of energy, and thought she might enjoy taking ballet lessons. Stephanie had loved ballet as a girl, so maybe Mia would, too. Mia's mother enrolled her in a dancing class.

"She was so petite, I thought she'd be ideal," Stephanie later said.

That's not quite the way it turned out. As far as Mia was concerned, dance class was too slow. It seemed that as soon as everyone in class started moving, the teacher would stop the dancing so that they could learn some other step. Besides, Mia didn't like wearing ballet slippers.

As she told a reporter years later, "I hated it. I lasted only one class."

Mia wanted to play soccer, just like the older Hamm kids. Her mother understood. She remembered that when she was growing up, there weren't many opportunities for girls to play sports. As she later recalled, "Those of us who wanted to be active found the joy in using our body in something like dance. Now they have this other option and it's beautiful." She put Mia's ballet shoes in a closet and bought her a tiny pair of soccer cleats and a pair of shin guards.

Mia waited and waited and waited until she turned five, when she could join a team of her own. Finally, Mia would get her chance to show what she could do on the field. She was one of the smallest and youngest players on the team, but that didn't matter. Nothing could stop Mia once she started. She had grown up with the game, and playing all those years against her bigger, older siblings had made her tougher and stronger than the rest of the kids. She understood how the game was supposed to be played. She could see the game develop better than most and although she was timid at first, she quickly discovered that once she started scoring goals, she didn't feel so shy anymore.

As she remembered later, "Soccer was a way to hang out and make friends."

In time, it would become much more than that.

CHAPTER TWO
1977–1986

CHOOSING SOCCER

The opportunity to play organized soccer wasn't the only event of 1977 that had a big impact on Mia's life: Bill and Stephanie decided to add a new member to the family. Mia's parents adopted an eight-year-old Asian American boy named Garrett. Garrett was an orphan and the Hamms had love to spare. It was a perfect match.

Soon, Mia and Garrett were nearly inseparable. He, too, loved to play soccer and other sports.

"He was an instant playmate for me," Mia said.

As Mia grew up, she tried to do everything Garrett did. "He let me hang out with him and his friends and play football, soccer, and basketball with them," she said.

Despite her small size, Mia was a good athlete. Garrett knew this, and called his little sister his "secret weapon" when the two would join his friends in the park for pickup games of baseball, football, basketball, and soccer.

"No one would want to pick me for their team," recalled Mia, "but Garrett would always pick me. We would downplay the fact that I was fast and could catch."

In the middle of the games, Garrett would give his secret weapon a look and Mia would start playing as hard as she could. One minute she was hanging back and the next she was running circles around the other children. She would get in behind the last defender to score the winning goal in soccer or catch the Hail Mary touchdown pass in football.

Playing against the older kids helped Mia improve her skills faster than other children her age. Soon she wasn't a secret weapon anymore. It didn't take long for everyone to figure out exactly how talented she was and learn to watch out for her.

In 1982, the World Cup was played. Mia was ten years old. The World Cup is the most important soccer competition in the world. It is played only every four years, and nearly every country wants its national team to qualify for the biggest soccer tournament on the planet. Qualification for each World

Cup is a four-year process of local, regional, and continental tournaments. Every country's national teams play most of their qualifying games during the summer, when professional leagues such as the Premier League, La Liga, Serie A, and the Bundesliga don't play games. They also play a few games during the fall, winter, and spring when all the professional leagues take short breaks called international breaks. The 1982 World Cup expanded the total number of teams involved from sixteen to twenty-four. The goal was to include more teams from across the globe not only to promote the game, but also to increase the level of play in the smaller, poorer countries.

The hope was that in the long run, this would make for better World Cup tournaments, but it also meant that the 1982 tournament would pair some World Cup powerhouse teams with some relative newcomers to international play. There were some blowouts during that tournament.

Although more and more children were playing soccer, very few Americans paid much attention to the 1982 World Cup. Except for a brief period in the mid-1970s when Pelé played in the North American

Soccer League, soccer had never been a popular spectator sport in America.

Part of the problem was that the American national team hadn't qualified for the World Cup since 1950. Most Americans didn't know the United States even had a national team, much less what the World Cup was. The United States was about the only country in the world that didn't televise the event. Everywhere else, the World Cup was like the Super Bowl, the World Series, the NBA Finals, and the Stanley Cup all wrapped up in one event. Billions of people worldwide stayed up late or woke up early to watch the World Cup matches on television, broadcasting live from the host country.

Mia was lucky, though. She lived in Wichita Falls, near the US-Mexico border, and they could pick up Mexican television broadcasts. In Mexico, soccer was extremely popular. The World Cup was huge. Television stations broadcast almost every game of the final rounds of the tournament, even when they took place on the other side of the world in the middle of the night.

The Hamm family watched as many games as they possibly could. Even though the announcers broadcast the games in Spanish, everyone in the family understood the game. As they watched the best players in the world, they discussed strategy and marveled at the athletes' skill. When they had a chance, Mia and the other Hamm children would race outside and try to imitate the players they had just watched.

The 1982 World Cup was won by Italy. They defeated West Germany 3–1 in the final game. It was the most important event in Mia's young life. She began to realize how the game of soccer could be played if played right, how creative the sport was, and what could be done with a soccer ball. She also became aware of just how big and important soccer was to people all over the world. It was more than the game she played with her friends. It was a worldwide phenomenon that could touch people, inspire nations, and unite enemies. She didn't yet pay much attention to the fact that every team in the World Cup was all male. She just knew that she wanted to play in a World Cup someday, too.

Despite the impact the World Cup had on Mia, she wasn't quite ready to turn her life over to soccer. After all, she was still a kid and enjoyed lots of different sports. She was good at every sport she chose to play. She wanted to play everything, and was one of the first girls in Wichita Falls to play Little League Baseball. She didn't know it, but even then she was a pioneer.

She even played football. When Mia was in seventh grade, a bunch of her friends were all excited about trying out for the school's junior high football team. They had all played football together on the playground. Mia knew she could throw and kick a football as well as any of her friends, male or female, and no one could run as fast as she could. When tryouts were announced, Mia signed up without hesitation. She had never noticed that girls didn't usually play football. Not until she went to practice did she realize she was the only girl trying to make the team.

"It was one of those things when you're young," she said later. "You really don't think boy-girl. They were my friends. They wanted me to play."

Being the only female trying out didn't stop her. Her friends told the coach she was a good player, and it didn't take long for the coach to learn that Mia's friends were right. She was so good that welcoming her to the team was an easy decision. She tried quarterback, but she usually played wide receiver and kicker. Her speed made her a real asset on the field.

As Mia grew older, her male friends kept growing taller and broader and she began to realize she was just too small to keep playing football. At the same time, it became increasingly clear that her best sport was soccer. She was a good basketball player and baseball player, an asset to the teams she played for. But on the soccer field, she was a star.

"I found I cared more about the results in soccer than in any other sport," Mia said.

On the soccer pitch, Mia usually played forward, striker, or winger. On offense, she'd streak down the sideline after the ball, then either cross the ball into the eighteen-yard box to a teammate or take the ball straight to the goal herself. When the other team had the ball, she usually formed the first line of defense. In order to move the ball past midfield and get in position to score, the opposition first had to get the ball past Mia.

The amazing Dutch soccer player Johan Cruyff once said, "In my teams, the goalie is the first attacker, and the striker the first defender."

Mia believed in the same philosophy. For many young athletes, the most difficult part about any sport is learning to anticipate the opponent's play, to know what is going to happen on the field before it actually happens. Because she played so much while so young, Mia developed that skill as a child. While most of her peers were still trying to figure out how to run full speed and control the ball at the same time, Mia did all of that instinctively, which allowed her to concentrate on the mental part of the game instead.

Before she even got the ball, she was thinking a play or two ahead of her teammates. That meant that when she received the ball, she already knew what she was going to do with it. If the defense eased up on her, anticipating a pass, she knew to take her defender on one-on-one and go to goal. If they pressed her, she instinctively knew where her teammates were going to be and how to get them the ball. Defenders soon learned that if they didn't focus on Mia, she could score at will. Two or three players were often assigned to cover her the entire game. But that didn't stop Mia. She realized that if two or three players were covering her, at least one teammate had to be wide open.

One of her favorite tricks was to run across the middle of the field with the ball to force several defenders to race after her. When they did, she'd spin and make a perfect pass between them to a wide-open teammate in front of the goal to allow him or her to score. She was so quick on the ball and so alert in the field that it almost appeared as if she was playing a different game, or at least at a different speed. By the time she was a teenager, she had graduated from the local youth leagues to club select teams made up of the best players from several communities. When she started playing on her high school team at Notre Dame High School in Wichita Falls, she decided to stop playing other sports in order to concentrate on soccer.

The stronger the competition, the better Mia played. She quickly developed from being just one of the best players in Wichita Falls to being the very best player in the state. And yet Mia didn't let it go to her head. She really didn't care whether she scored or not, as long as her team won. Meanwhile, women's soccer and women's sports in general were getting more popular. Throughout the 1970s and early 1980s, people began to realize that women had just as much of a right to play sports as men. There was no physical reason for them not to play. The United States government even recognized that fact and ruled that school sports programs had to treat male and female athletes equally. Known as Title IX, the regulation directed public schools and universities to expand their sports programs to introduce more teams for girls and young women.

Many high schools and universities started women's soccer teams. Women were even being offered college scholarships to play soccer. Beginning in 1982, the National Collegiate Athletic Association, also known as the NCAA, started a collegiate national championship tournament. That same year, the United States selected its first national women's soccer team to compete in international tournaments. The United States was finally catching up to the rest of the world: women's soccer had already been an established sport for a decade or more in most European countries. Millions of young girls and women around the world now played soccer, and thousands more were beginning to play each year. Now it was the United States' turn.

Mia was playing soccer at just the right time. Opportunities for female soccer players were expanding rapidly. Women's soccer clubs were talking about someday holding a women's World Cup tournament, and there was a growing movement to include women's and men's soccer in the Olympic Games.

In 1985, when Mia was just thirteen years old, she

was a Texas All-State selection in women's soccer. The selection qualified her to play in several big tournaments and all-star games. At one such game, John Cossaboon, coach of the fledgling United States women's soccer Olympic development team, was in the stands. He wasn't really scouting for his own team but instead was looking for good players he could recommend to college coaches. He was hoping the college teams would develop them into good players who just might make it to the Olympic team. Cossaboon and his assistant coaches attended dozens of games each year.

As soon as he started watching, he noticed Mia Hamm. She was all over the field, stripping the ball from her opponents on defense and dominating possession on offense, setting up her teammates with perfectly weighted passes and making aggressive moves to the goal. After only a few moments, it became obvious to Cossaboon that even on a team of all-stars, she was light-years better than every other player. No one else on the field had her speed or feel for the game. No one else had her touch on the ball. She could rocket passes through traffic or gently set a ball on her teammates' feet.

She was tough, too! Where other players sometimes hesitated to make a tackle or tried to avoid contact, Mia was willing to make the hard shoulder challenge, while keeping it clean. She didn't think twice about running headlong into a crowd for the ball. She wanted it more than the other players on the field, and she often stripped the ball from players who had much better position than she did. Cossaboon couldn't believe it when he learned that Mia was only thirteen. She was the youngest player on the field and already the best by far. He had high standards, and thought that she was still a little raw and had a lot to learn but also had potential to shine.

When Cossaboon looked at Mia, he saw the future of women's soccer in the United States. Without hesitation, he asked Mia to join the Olympic development team. He told Bill and Stephanie Hamm that Mia was already good enough to get a college scholarship.

Mia was dumbfounded. She had never really thought about playing soccer much beyond high school, let alone someday having a chance to play in the Olympic Games. Now all of a sudden she knew what she wanted to do.

She wanted to be a soccer player. No one could tell her that sports were just for boys anymore.

CHAPTER THREE
1987

A MEMBER OF THE TEAM

Mia's life changed when she joined the Olympic development team. Soccer had been a game she played for fun and enjoyed, but now it was getting much more serious. Next to her family, it was the most important thing in her life.

Being a member of the development team gave Mia a chance to travel all around the country and play soccer with and against the best young American players. Some girls her age might have had a difficult time doing that without getting homesick, but Mia was prepared. Her family had moved several times as she was growing up, so she was accustomed to meeting new people and adjusting to new situations. She was still shy, but had learned that soccer was a good way to make friends.

Once again, the stronger the competition she faced, the better she seemed to play. After only one year with Mia on his team, Coach Cossaboon knew that it would soon be time for her to move on. She was improving rapidly and he wanted to make sure she was allowed to reach her full potential.

Cossaboon contacted Anson Dorrance, coach of both the University of North Carolina women's soccer team and the US women's national team. He told Dorrance that there was a player he had to see.

In the world of American women's soccer, Dorrance was famous. On the UNC campus in Chapel Hill, North Carolina, he was as admired as Dean Smith, the legendary coach of the men's basketball team. Smith even admitted as much, once telling an out-of-town reporter that the basketball team wasn't such a big deal around Chapel Hill, because UNC "was really a girls' soccer school."

Dorrance had attended and played soccer for UNC, and he began his collegiate coaching career with the UNC men's team in 1976, a position he held through 1989. When UNC decided to create a varsity women's team in 1979, Dorrance took on that task as well.

Dorrance was a tough taskmaster who demanded results. At first, he tried to coach the women just as he did the men. He soon learned that didn't work very well. Dorrance eventually came to the conclusion that he had to take a different approach to the women's team. Female players, he discovered, had to trust him before they would carry out his instructions. He stopped yelling so much and started teaching. "With women, if you want to get the most out of them, they have to feel you relate personally to them," he later said in an interview. Incorporating his new approach, Dorrance discovered that "there is a genuine team cohesiveness among great women's teams because they have a greater capacity to relate to each other than we do as males."

Before long, his women's team was even more successful than his men's squad. Dorrance enjoyed his new task so much that he eventually gave up his post as the men's coach to focus on the women's team full-time. The UNC women's team became one of the greatest dynasties in the history of college sports.

They rarely lost a game. In 1982, they captured the first NCAA women's soccer championship and four of the next five titles. In 1986, based on his unparalleled record of success, Dorrance was also named coach of the US women's national team. No one in the country knew more about women's soccer or female soccer players than Dorrance.

Although women's soccer was much more established in Europe, Asia, and South America, Dorrance set out to create the best women's soccer team in the world. His position as national team coach gave him the opportunity to see the best soccer players on the field. He knew that if the United States was ever going to compete at the international level, he had to have the very best players on the team. During the off-season, he traveled the country in search of those select few young women. No young player he had seen before, male or female, made as strong an impression on him as Mia Hamm did that first time he saw her play. Dorrance got his first look at Mia in 1987, when she played for a US under-19 team at a national tournament in New Orleans, Louisiana.

Dorrance watched Mia closely from the sidelines, and later remembered, "She was playing right half-back. I watched her take a seven-yard run at the ball, and I said, 'Oh, my gosh!' I'd never seen speed like that in the women's game. She had unlimited potential...she had an incredible ability to shred defenders and get to the goal."

Like Cossaboon, Dorrance wanted to make sure that soccer remained a challenge to Mia, so that she would continue to grow as a player. Despite her obvious skill and talent, the international game was far more difficult than the one Mia had been playing. Thus far, she had relied on her physical ability to succeed against players who were less talented and experienced, but she would need to improve her technical skills to compete on a global stage.

In international play every player was fast and strong, and many had more experience than Mia. In order to make certain Mia's game continued to develop to its full potential, Dorrance realized he had to expose her to the US national team. He asked her to participate in an upcoming training camp and try out for the team. Even if she didn't make it, she would learn what it would take for her to reach the next level and it would give her something to shoot for.

Mia accepted the invitation immediately. She was excited by the opportunity, but she was also very, very nervous. Most of the team were either in college or had recently graduated. Mia Hamm was only fifteen years old.

She was nervous, shy, and a little intimidated. A few days before, she was playing on good teams, but during the national team camp she was playing with players such as striker Michelle Akers, whom many people considered to be the best women's soccer player in the world. At Mia's first meeting with the team, they all spent several hours in the gym, working out with weights and other fitness equipment. Mia had never spent much time in the gym before. She'd just played soccer. The long workout left her exhausted. "I thought I'd die," she remembered later. Then she got the surprise of her young life. After working out in the gym, the squad headed outside for practice! She spent another two hours on the field, going through drills and scrimmages with the team. At the end of the day, all she wanted to do was sleep. Her thighs throbbed, and she felt as if her entire body was going to go into one huge cramp. She had never worked so hard in her life.

Yet she couldn't fall asleep. Every time she closed her eyes, she saw herself playing soccer on the national team. She was more excited about playing soccer than she had ever been before. The players on the team were so good, they made Mia reassess her entire approach to soccer. Up to that point in her life, soccer had been important to her and she had cared about winning or losing, but she had never felt that losing was the end of the world. As a female athlete, she had been conditioned to care less about winning than male athletes did. On the national team, everything was different.

"I loved how competitive it was," she said later. "I was like, 'Wow. Look how hard these players work.'"

The captain of the national team, April Heinrichs, made a big impression on Mia. "[April] just wanted to win, and for a female wanting that, it was just so new. I realized I had to do a lot of stuff on my own if I wanted to stay on this team."

Mia was also amazed by the other players' grasp of the game. As she later recalled, she realized that "tactically, I didn't have a clue. I had no idea how to play," at least at the international level. She knew little about the subtleties of strategy and playing together as a team with players who were as skilled as she was.

When Mia returned home after the camp, she was laser-focused on playing soccer. She now knew exactly what she wanted out of the game of soccer, and she made it her life's goal.

"She came back from camp," said her father, "and said she wanted to do two things. Go to North Carolina [to play for Dorrance at UNC] and win the world championship." She had become best friends with one of her teammates on the under-19 team, Kristine Lilly, and the two girls dreamed of going off together to UNC and playing on the national team.

Mia's dream soon started to come true when Dorrance named her to the US national team. In August of 1987, Mia accompanied the squad to China, where they were scheduled to play two games against the Chinese women's national team.

Even for an experienced traveler like Mia, the trip to China was a big deal, but Mia was most excited about getting an opportunity to play with the US team. She made her first appearance for the United States in the first game against China, on August 3, 1987, in Tianjin. There were thousands of fans in the stands, way more than Mia had ever played in front of before.

She didn't start, but came on as a substitute. She was so nervous, her few moments on the field went by in a blur. While she was confident in her skills on offense, she wasn't so sure about her defensive play. On the international level, defense is vital. Because all the players are so talented, a single goal is often the difference in a game. Mia was still learning her defensive responsibilities and wasn't confident in her ability to read the other team's runs or in her abilities to mark opposing players.

All she could think about was trying not to mess up. And although she didn't score a goal or play particularly well, she didn't blow it, either. She had survived her first game in international competition and the United States won 2–0. With that out of the way, Mia could focus on getting more playing time.

At the time, Mia was what coaches referred to as a "project," a player with vast potential who needed time to learn, develop, and grow. Coach Dorrance, although he wanted to win every game the team played, was already looking toward the future. He hoped that in a few years, FIFA, the international organization that runs soccer, would agree to hold a women's World Cup tournament. Dorrance knew that by the time that took place, some of his best players on the current team would likely be too old to play. He needed young players like Mia to start playing in his system now, so that they would be ready to contribute when the Women's World Cup was finally held. He knew it would take time for Mia to become a force on the team, full of growing pains and mistakes, but he believed in her and her talents.

In the meantime, Mia still had to finish high school. After all, she was only in the tenth grade.

After her sophomore year, her father gathered the family and told them some important news. Bill Hamm, who was now a colonel in the air force, was being transferred again. The Hamm family was going to move from Texas to Northern Virginia.

It was a stressful time for everyone in the family. A few years before, Mia's brother Garrett had been diagnosed with a disease called aplastic anemia, a blood disorder that caused his body to fail to produce enough platelets. Garrett and Mia were partners in crime and very close, so it was a tough time for her. Garrett, whom Mia had always looked up to and considered the best athlete in the family, had to stop playing sports. Although he continued to lead an almost normal life, the illness was progressive and a source of constant concern.

Mia didn't know what to think about the move to Northern Virginia. Although she was accustomed to moving around a lot, she didn't want to leave her friends at school and have to start all over again. Then she realized that the move would bring her closer to the other members of the national team, many of whom also played for Dorrance at the University of North Carolina, and that she wouldn't have to spend as much time away from her family as before when she went to train with the national team. Besides, even though she would miss her old friends, she now knew that being part of a team meant she would always have friends nearby. "You move and have new friends as soon as you join a team," she said. In the coming years, she would be making friends all over the world.

CHAPTER FOUR
1988–1989

FROM SHOOTING STAR TO TAR HEEL

The Hamms moved to Burke, Virginia, in time for Mia to enroll in Lake Braddock High School in the fall of 1988. Once they got settled, the family quickly discovered that Northern Virginia and the suburbs around Washington, DC, were a hotbed of women's soccer. It didn't take long for Mia to find a new team. In fact, she joined two teams.

Lake Braddock High had a strong soccer program. In 1987, the girls' team won the Virginia AAA-division state championship. In the spring of 1988, they were heavily favored to repeat, but lost in overtime to archrival Woodbridge in the finals.

The school's academics were just as important to Mia. She knew the national team would soon take up a great deal of her time. So after discussions with her parents and the administration at Lake Braddock High, she decided to accelerate her academic program. The plan was to simultaneously complete both her junior and senior years. The fact that Coach Dorrance had offered her a scholarship to play soccer at UNC was another incentive for her to finish high school as soon as she could. She couldn't wait to get to Chapel Hill.

In Virginia, soccer was a spring sport, so Mia joined a club team, the Braddock Road Shooting Stars. The Stars were one of the best junior girls' soccer clubs in the country, and she got to play with several of her Lake Braddock classmates.

It was a hectic year. Mia spent most of her time studying, working out, and playing soccer. Unlike many girls her age, she rarely dated or attended dances. There just wasn't enough time.

When spring came, the Lake Braddock girls' soccer team started their season as the favorites to win the state championship.

Mia was not a secret to other teams in Northern Virginia. After playing with the Shooting Stars and training with the national team, Mia had been pegged as one of the best players in the state. Coach Carolyn Rice looked forward to having that much talent on the Lake Braddock High Bruins.

Coming into an established team can be an unnerving experience. Sometimes established players resent new players, particularly those as talented as Mia. Although Mia was looking forward to playing, she knew there might be some ruffled feathers while the team went through the transition of bringing her into the fold. The Bruins were already loaded with talent. Eight of eleven starters had returned from the previous season. Even though Mia knew several teammates from the Shooting Stars and had met everyone else during her first semester at Lake Braddock, she still worried about fitting in on the field.

When practice started, Coach Rice and the Bruin players soon discovered that Mia was an even better player than they had thought. The best part about having Mia on the team wasn't the way she played—it was the way she acted.

"The thing that stands out about Mia," Coach Rice later told a reporter, "is her attention to the details of every task. She works hard to push herself, but by her own actions, she also motivates and encourages the others to work even harder."

Mia didn't have an attitude. If anything, she downplayed her own accomplishments and was modest to a fault. Her experience with the national team had taught her the importance of team chemistry. Before long, her teammates didn't look at her as someone new, but rather as a member of the Bruin soccer family. She had become their friend, and a teammate in every sense of the word.

Coach Rice installed Mia on the team's front line with two established star players, Colette Cunningham and Liz Pike. Soon the three talented girls were dominating women's soccer in the state of Virginia.

The Washington Post / contributor / Getty Images

MIA ON THE BALL IN FRONT OF THE GOAL FOR LAKE BRADDOCK

Despite the fact that every opponent was gunning for them, the Bruins raced through the bulk of their season undefeated. Late in the year they stumbled, losing games to Woodson and West Springfield. As Coach Rice commented later, the losses only made the Bruins more determined to win the state championship.

"They knew what they did wrong," Coach Rice said at the time. "I didn't have to tell them."

In their last few regular-season games, the team got back on track and qualified for the state tournament. In the semifinals, Mia scored two goals in a 5–1 win over Monacan. That set up a rematch from the year before between Lake Braddock and Woodbridge in the finals on May 27.

Woodbridge assigned their best defender, Susan Braun, to mark Mia. Although Braun wasn't as quick as Mia, she was a smart player who worked hard to cut off the passing lanes to Mia's teammates, limiting her touches on the ball. But no one on the field had Mia's skills and experience. She made the most of her few opportunities.

Fourteen minutes into the game, the score was 0–0. Then Mia got in behind the Woodbridge defense.

Woodbridge had possession of the ball near mid-field when a Lake Braddock player forced a turn-over. Without hesitating, Mia made a run toward the Woodbridge goal, looking for the ball.

Her quick burst took Braun by surprise, and Mia's teammate hit her with a perfect chip pass. Mia took a few touches and used her speed to push the ball toward the goal. Only one defender stood between her and the goalkeeper.

As Coach Dorrance had previously noticed, no one got by defenders better than Mia. She raced straight toward the Woodbridge player, then faked and cut to the side, leaving the befuddled girl stumbling and trying to change direction. By the time she did, Mia was already several yards past her and in the clear.

Woodbridge goalie Erin Tierney had no chance. From just outside the penalty box, Mia blasted a shot past Tierney's outstretched arms into the right corner of the net. Mia's teammates mobbed her, screaming and cheering. Best of all, Lake Braddock led 1–0.

But Woodbridge fought back. Over the next twenty minutes, neither team scored as Braun recovered to contain Mia.

At the forty-one-minute mark, Mia got the ball

again, deep in the Lake Braddock defensive third on the right flank.

The sight of Mia Hamm on the ball driving to goal caused confusion in the Woodbridge defense. Another player joined Braun, and they tried to force Mia into the corner.

That was a mistake. Mia knew that somewhere a Bruin player was now open.

She spotted Colette Cunningham in front of the goal. Mia stutter-stepped and created a narrow gap between her two defenders. Before they could close in, she rocketed a cross pass to Cunningham.

Cunningham shot from twelve yards out and the ball found the left corner of the net, putting Lake Braddock up by two.

The goal broke Woodbridge's spirit. Mia later scored a second goal, and the Bruins went on to win 4–1 and lead Lake Braddock to another state championship.

Mia didn't have much time to celebrate, however. The next day she and her two front-line teammates, Pike and Cunningham, played in a tournament game for the Shooting Stars. Each of the three Braddock High girls scored two goals as the team destroyed a Canadian team, 8–0.

Shooting Stars coach Denise Mishalow remarked after the game, "My job isn't too difficult. All I have to do is put them on the field and let them play."

A few weeks later, Mia graduated from high school. She rejoined the national team just in time to travel to Sardinia, Italy, where they played Poland to a 0–0 tie. Then it was time to prepare for college. Mia was on her way to Chapel Hill and the University of North Carolina. She was about to be a Tar Heel.

CHAPTER FIVE
1989–1990

NATIONAL CHAMPION

Mia was thrilled to be going to the University of North Carolina, but like most teenagers who go away to college, she knew she would miss her family.

Her situation was made doubly difficult because her father was again transferred, this time back to Italy. Although she had done a lot of traveling, Mia had never been so far from her parents for such a long period of time.

It helped that she already knew Coach Dorrance and many of her teammates. Her good friend Kristine Lilly was also a freshman at UNC. Her college teammates soon became like a second family to Mia.

Still, Mia was under a lot of pressure at UNC. She decided to study political science, a major that was demanding. Classes were tough. Even though Mia was used to working hard at school, college-level work was much more difficult than her high school assignments had been.

Her commitments to the soccer team proved a challenge as well. College soccer season takes place in the fall, so as soon as school started, so too did the soccer season. In addition to practices, all members of the team were expected to attend weight or cardio training. They also played a lot of games, which meant they did a lot of traveling.

Mia knew she was considered the team's most promising new recruit. The Tar Heels had gone undefeated since their loss in the 1985 NCAA championship game and had won three straight NCAA championships since. She knew Coach Dorrance would be dissatisfied with anything less than another national title. Mia didn't want to let him or her new teammates down, but on a squad of so many good players, including two-time NCAA Player of the Year Shannon Higgins, Mia wasn't quite sure she'd even get a chance to play. She knew the older girls on the team wouldn't have patience with what they referred to as "freshman mistakes."

While Mia later admitted that she felt insecure about her play that season, her performance on the field spoke otherwise. She made the already powerful Tar Heel attack one of the most explosive in the history of collegiate women's soccer, despite playing in the Atlantic Coast Conference (ACC), one of the most competitive conferences in the nation.

The Tar Heels began the season ranked number one in the country, but they played a tough schedule. Three other ACC teams, North Carolina State, Virginia, and Duke, were also ranked in the top twenty. Still, the Tar Heels tore through the regular season, dispatching most opponents with ease. Higgins directed the attack as the general in the midfield. Mia teamed up with fellow freshman Kristine Lilly to provide more than an ample scoring punch from the forward line. This strong offense, combined with a staunch high-pressure defense, made the team a nightmare matchup for every other school. On a late-season road trip, the longest in school history, the Tar Heels faced three top-twenty teams from the West Coast—Santa Clara, St. Mary's, and Stanford—and defeated all three without allowing a single goal. Heading into the ACC championship tournament, UNC had a twelve-game winning streak and had outscored the opposition 77–6.

The Tar Heels knew they couldn't afford to take the tournament for granted. If they didn't focus on every game, they could easily lose one or more, and it could cost them the conference title. Despite winning the national title in 1988, they had lost the ACC championship in the conference tournament the previous season to their fiercest rivals, the Wolfpack of North Carolina State, on penalty kicks following a 1–1 tie. UNC lost the league title in heartbreaking fashion that year. While the tie and standoff had preserved their unbeaten record, it had provided little satisfaction for the Tar Heels, and NC State had all the bragging rights.

For the second consecutive year, UNC faced the Wolfpack in the finals of the ACC tournament. It was time for some payback. The Tar Heels cruised into the conference tournament with twenty-one wins, no losses, and one tie. The Tar Heels were the heavy favorites to beat the Wolfpack. Coach Dorrance was confident, but cautious. Although he admitted that the 1989 Tar Heels were "the most exciting team we've ever had," Dorrance felt he needed to manage the expectations of those who considered his team a dynasty. Wins didn't come for free; North Carolina still had to play the game.

"We're only a dynasty in the sense that we've worked hard," he said. "We have strived for a goal and are reaching it."

For the first time all year, the Tar Heel defense was surprisingly porous and let in three goals. Fortunately, Mia Hamm and Kristine Lilly were up to the challenge. Each player tallied two goals as UNC beat NC State 5–3. Mia Hamm, a freshman and the youngest player on the field, was named the most valuable player of the ACC tournament.

Both UNC and NC State qualified for the NCAA tournament. After UNC blasted Hartford 9–0 in the quarterfinals, the Tar Heels were set to take on NC State in the semifinals. The Wolfpack was all that stood between the Tar Heels and another appearance in the finals. The Tar Heels needed another win.

On a team of veterans, no one proved more adept at handling the pressure of the tournament than Mia. In the first half, the game was scoreless when she picked up a loose ball just outside the penalty area and blasted a shot past the goalie to put UNC ahead, 1–0. Then, just ninety seconds into the second half, Kristine Lilly also scored. The Tar Heels defense then shut down the Wolfpack and held NC State scoreless on their way to a 2–0 win and a berth in the NCAA championship game.

They faced Colorado College in the finals. Shannon

Higgins demonstrated why she had once again been named Player of the Year. Incredibly, for the fourth year in a row, she scored the game-winning goal in the NCAA finals. The Tar Heels won 2–0 and captured their fourth straight NCAA title.

Shannon Higgins and Kristine Lilly garnered most of the headlines that season, but Mia Hamm led the team in goals scored with twenty-one. And still she wasn't satisfied. She knew that most observers considered her primarily an offensive player whose all-around skills were just a notch below those of her more illustrious teammates. She vowed to make some major improvements in the off-season.

She decided to work on her conditioning. During training camp in the summer of 1990 with the national team, she peppered Coach Dorrance with questions about strategy and ways she could improve her game. She wanted to make certain the UNC dynasty continued. Their conversations led to a number of game-changing insights.

In their first game of the summer, the United States took on Norway, one of the best teams in the world, and Mia scored her first goal in international competition. The US national team went on to have their most successful season to date, winning all six games they played. The best news for 1991 was FIFA's announcement that they would start planning the first Women's World Cup tournament ever. Mia was thrilled. Maybe she would get to play in the World Cup like her heroes did in 1982.

Mia returned to Chapel Hill in the fall, ready for another winning season. But many observers thought the UNC women's soccer program had peaked. The loss of Shannon Higgins and several other experienced graduating seniors left the Tar Heels with one of their youngest teams since the program had begun in 1979. Mia had grown accustomed to being one of the youngest members of every team she had played for, but now she was considered a veteran. Her teammates started to look to her for leadership.

At the beginning of the 1990 season, the Tar Heels picked up right where they had left off the season before, but a road game against the University of Connecticut on September 22 would throw a wrench in their plans for another undefeated season.

It was a close game from the first whistle. The two teams battled back and forth, each team giving up goals before pulling one back. In the end, the Tar Heels lost in an overtime thriller, 3–2. That loss ended the team's amazing unbeaten streak at a remarkable 103 straight games. After the game, the UConn players piled up on one another and hundreds of fans raced onto the field to celebrate. UNC left the field in an unfamiliar position: defeated. This shook the team's confidence. They were a young team and how they bounced back from this setback would color their entire season.

Soccer fans all over the country were shocked by the loss and some of Mia's own teammates were devastated. The team was accustomed to winning and dominating their opponents. In those 103 games, the Tar Heels had trailed for only 19 minutes and 45 seconds out of 9,270 minutes of play.

The pressure to win may have been part of the reason they lost. When the team realized they couldn't shake the UConn team, some of Mia's teammates felt rattled and started to press for a goal. Mia was one of the few players who had kept her focus, and it paid off with both of the Tar Heels' goals.

A week later, UNC was back in trouble. Despite facing a young George Mason University team that had won only twice all year, the powerful Tar Heels continued their poor play. It appeared as if the loss to UConn had caused the team to begin to doubt itself. Perhaps the dynasty was over.

For eighty-nine minutes, the two teams played to a 0–0 tie. George Mason goalie Hollis Kosco, normally a defender, played the game of her life, making nineteen saves. UNC's best chance to score had come in the forty-eighth minute, when Mia's twenty-five-yard rocket had rattled off the crossbar.

Late in the game, many Tar Heel players began to press again and they botched several chances to put the ball in the back of the net. With only fifteen seconds left in the game, Mia took over.

As a George Mason defender tried to control the ball at midfield and pass out of pressure, Mia charged in and cut off the pass. Then she took off down the left wing as the fans at George Mason's home field stood and yelled.

Mia went straight to goal and the keeper came off her line, trying to close down Mia's shooting angle. But Mia's experience proved critical. She slowed and waited as the goalie approached, biding her time. Mia faked a shot, got Kosco to commit, cut the ball onto her other foot, and in a blur flicked the ball to the opposite side. Kosco dove for the ball, but the slow-rolling shot found the back of the net—with only eight seconds left on the clock.

Mia's teammates mobbed her. She had stayed calm when everyone else had panicked. All Mia would say after the game about her winning shot was "I guessed right," but her teammates and coach knew better. She had become a leader of the Tar Heels that day.

Even Mia understood that. "I think I have a different role than I did last year," she said later. "I'm one of the more experienced players on the field now."

Dorrance was effusive in his praise. "She has the best acceleration of any player that plays the game right now in the world. Once she gets shoulder to shoulder with you, unless you pull her jersey or foul her, she's going to go by you."

The last-second win had brought the team together. They had proven to themselves that they could weather any low point the season might throw at them and grind out a tough win. They soon returned to their usual dominating style of play. Only now they looked to Mia to lead them. And she did—straight to the conference finals.

Will McIntyre / contributor / Getty Images

MIA CUTTING THE BALL BACK ON A DEFENDER

In the ACC tournament finals, the number-one Tar Heels faced number-three Virginia Cavaliers. In the first half, a scoreless tie, the Cavaliers outshot the Tar Heels and controlled play. This time, no one on the North Carolina team panicked. After all, they had a not-so-secret weapon: Mia Hamm.

Early in the second half, the ball rolled out of bounds on the Virginia end and North Carolina was awarded a corner kick. Mia placed the ball on the ground, took a few steps back, and looked toward the goal as her teammates jockeyed for position in front of the net. She took a deep breath and stepped quickly toward the ball, kicking it so that it spun sideways through the air and curved toward the goal.

As the shot rocketed in front of the goal, players from both teams jumped and tried to head the ball. The goalie leaped into the air, but she misjudged the ball's position. It sailed over her hands, continuing to curve. No one touched it. Like a hawk coming in for the kill, the ball swooped down and hooked into the far corner.

Olimpico! One of the greatest and most difficult goals to score is a goal directly from a corner kick, the Olympic goal better known as an Olimpico. And Mia scored a beauty in one of the biggest games of her career. UNC led 1–0. Late in the game on another corner kick by Mia, Tar Heel Paige Coley headed home another goal to cement a comfortable 2–0 win.

"All I'm trying to do is get it in the vicinity of the [penalty] box," Mia said, downplaying her shot. When pressed by a reporter to say more, a modest Mia deferred, saying, "There's nothing more to say about it."

In the NCAA tournament, UNC blasted through the competition and reached the finals easily. The best part was that the finals were scheduled to be played at Fetzer Field on the University of North Carolina campus, and the Tar Heels were going to play UConn, the team that had ended their winning streak. It was the perfect final for UNC—they'd be on their home turf and have the chance to prove they could win against the only team to defeat them that season.

This was a different Tar Heels team from the one that had lost that streak-breaking game. They were tougher. Physically they were stronger. Mentally they were tempered steel. Mia had not only grown into a great leader, but her play had improved as well.

The UConn Huskies knew they had to shut Mia

down if they were going to have a chance at repeating their win. That meant keeping the ball from her and double-teaming her when she did get the ball. But as Mia learned as a kid, if two defenders were focused on her, that meant one of her teammates would be wide open. In this game, that teammate was Kristine Lilly, who scored two first-half goals. The Tar Heels dominated on offense, outshooting the Huskies 14–4. UNC put the game away in the second half by scoring four more times and limiting Connecticut to only three shots. The Tar Heels won their fifth straight NCAA title in a blowout.

One UConn player called the Tar Heels' play "the best performance of soccer I've seen in my college career."

Mia spelled out the Tar Heels' approach to the game. "Coach told us to remember who we are and what it means to play for North Carolina," she said. "We wanted to bury them psychologically in the first fifteen minutes, and that's exactly what we did."

Although Mia was thrilled with the victory and had led the NCAA in scoring with twenty-four goals, the end of the season was bittersweet. As she walked across the campus after the game, with the trees blazing in full fall color, she tried to soak it all in and enjoy the moment. In only a few weeks, it would all be over. In order to continue to play for the national team and participate in the first Women's World Cup, Mia Hamm would have to quit school. To make her World Cup dream a reality, she would have to give up being a Tar Heel.

CHAPTER SIX
1991

THE WORLD CUP

The first-ever Women's World Cup was billed as the biggest event in women's soccer. Though the level of play of the US women's national team was rapidly improving since it played its first game in 1985, it still lagged behind that of many other nations whose women's programs predated that of the United States. The six straight American wins in the summer of 1990 had come against teams that were not at full strength and weren't a good indicator of how well the team was actually going to play in the 1991 World Cup.

Many European countries had a strong system of club teams, which allowed female players to hone their skills against the best players in the country all year round. Japan even had a professional women's league. Some nations paid their players livable salaries, which allowed the players the luxury of playing soccer full-time. Although a few American women such as Michelle Akers played overseas, after an American female soccer player graduated from college there was no place in the United States to play at a professional level, and no one to play against. The Americans were at an extreme disadvantage.

If the US team was to catch up with the top teams, it had to do so quickly. The Americans had less than a year to come together as a team, qualify for the tournament, and, if they did, play well in the actual World Cup. Between mandatory practices, training camps, tournaments, and so-called friendlies (exhibition matches against teams from other nations in which the results don't count), the process of reaching the World Cup left the players no time to do anything else, such as having a job or going to school.

In exchange for their commitment to the team, the players didn't receive a salary, only room and board. But there was another benefit: the satisfaction of knowing they were doing everything possible to win the Cup and promote the cause of women's soccer throughout the United States and the world. Everyone on the national team knew that the first World Cup was going to be historic, and the American women wanted to leave a mark on the tournament. And if they were fortunate enough to win, the United States Soccer Federation (USSF), the governing body that controls soccer in the United States, promised the women a $50,000 award to be divided equally among the members of the team.

Their male counterparts on the men's US national team had it much easier. They were paid a salary, received far more support from the USSF than the women's team did, and got to stay in hotels on the road. The women, on the other hand, were often housed in barrack-like hostels or in private homes. Yet despite the inequity, most members of the team willingly gave up their jobs, left their families, put off marrying, postponed having children, and/or left college in order to follow their dreams.

Although Mia later called her decision to leave UNC "the hardest thing I've ever had to do," at the same time she was excited. She knew she could go back to college and the Tar Heels team after the tournament was over if she redshirted, so she took a year off to prepare for the World Cup. For an entire year, playing soccer would be her full-time occupation. Mia knew she needed that time to work on becoming as strong on defense as she was on offense.

The team of sixteen players and several alternates

first got together in January for five days of intensive training camp, followed by a similar camp in February. In late March, they came together once more to prepare for a big tournament in Bulgaria.

For the next nine months, they spent virtually every moment together. They trained together, ate together, lived together. For some this might seem like too much, but for these women it only worked to make them closer. They learned one another's habits and tendencies. This would prove invaluable when the teammates played on the field together.

The intense schedule also worked to the team's advantage. Many European teams didn't start playing together full-time until the club leagues ended in the spring. No matter how talented they were as individuals, it still took time to learn to play together.

The Americans, on the other hand, bonded quickly. Nearly half the team had once played for Dorrance at North Carolina, so they were already familiar with his system and with one another.

That didn't mean it would be easy. Because of injuries to other players, Mia had to adapt to a different position on the national team. She had always played forward in high school and college, but on the national team she played right midfielder, a position with greater defensive responsibilities. On offense, her primary duty was to be a playmaker, feeding the ball to her team's forwards. While she would still have opportunities to score goals herself, they would have to come within the team's offensive tactics.

The change had the exact effect Mia had hoped for when she joined the team. It forced her to elevate her game and use a wider variety of skills than she was accustomed to at North Carolina.

For the first time in her life, Mia actually had to battle for a place on the team. Dorrance wasn't reserving a spot on the team for anyone. If a player didn't produce, there were several alternates willing to take her place. The competition was fierce, but it was also good-natured and supportive.

The team played well together in Bulgaria and gained confidence, winning five matches in seven days, all shutouts, against teams from the host country, the USSR, Yugoslavia, Hungary, and France. As soon as they returned to the United States, they were on the road once more, this time to Haiti. There, they had to play a round-robin tournament against other North American and Caribbean countries in order to qualify for the World Cup's final round of sixteen teams.

They won all five games with ease, shutting out all five opponents and scoring an amazing forty-seven goals. Something special was brewing in America.

The team followed by touring Europe in May and playing five friendlies, against France, England, Holland, Denmark, and Germany. They won three of five games. The two losses alarmed everyone on the team. They knew they would have to play much better to have a chance to win the Cup. They were good, but they weren't good enough—at least not yet.

The team spent most of June and July in training camp before traveling to China for a series of three friendlies against the Chinese. They returned to the United States with only a single victory.

Things didn't get much better when they played host to two pairs of friendlies against Norway and China in the United States. Both visiting teams were expected to do well in the World Cup finals and they were a good test for the US team. The United States lost twice to Norway and split with China. In their last twelve games against international competition, their record was a lackluster 5–6–1.

When the team traveled to China for the World Cup finals in mid-November, no one expected the United States to do very well. Yet despite their record, the US team members never stopped believing in themselves and were cautiously optimistic.

The Americans' recent losses had given them a clear picture of how they needed to improve. They seemed to play better when they played aggressively and attacked the goal. When they sat back and let the other team determine the pace of the game, they struggled to contain the opposition. In other words, they learned firsthand that the best defense is a good offense. With several key players nursing injuries, they hadn't been at full strength earlier in the fall. Going into the finals, just about everyone was healthy.

Mia had adjusted well to midfield. She discovered that her acceleration, which had served her so well at forward, was even more useful in the middle of the pack. And at five foot five and 125 pounds, she was strong enough to mark other players and fast enough to close in on attackers quickly. She found that she could track most of her opponents, and if they made a mistake and lost control of the ball, she could instantly turn to the offensive side of her game and force the play downfield. It was a bonus that her North Carolina teammate Kristine Lilly had also decided to take a leave from school to play with the squad. She played opposite Mia at left mid-field, and the two players knew they could depend on each other.

The team's offense focused on striker Michelle Akers, a member of the team since 1985 and widely considered one of the best players in the world. Strong and aggressive, the five-foot-ten-inch Akers had the hardest shot in women's soccer. One coach, a former professional goalie himself, said her shots were "like cannonballs when you catch them."

As the youngest player on the team, Mia looked up to her teammates, particularly Akers. "Usually she draws a crowd of defenders around her," said Mia when asked to describe a typical Akers goal, "and when she gets the ball, she turns and gets hit, then she turns again and gets hit again, then she claws her way through the pack, calms herself, and strikes the ball perfectly. She's so composed and focused."

The Americans played their first World Cup game on November 17, 1991, against a tough Swed-ish team. They went into the game knowing that a single loss would probably be enough to prevent them from getting out of first-round play and into the knockout round.

After a hard-fought contest, the Americans won

3–2 in an upset, and Mia scored the winning goal in the sixty-second minute. Then they defeated Brazil 5–0 two days later. They followed with two more wins, the first a 3–0 win against Japan and then a 7–0 victory against Taiwan, a game in which Akers scored an amazing five goals. When they took the field against Germany on November 27 for a highly anticipated semifinal matchup, they were just one game away from reaching the finals. They had already done better than most had predicted, and few expected the Americans to make it through the semifinals.

Riding a wave of emotion, the Americans swamped the German team 5–2. Their aggressive play had made the difference. With Mia Hamm and Kristine Lilly challenging every ball and forcing play back toward the German goal, the Germans simply couldn't get out of their defensive third.

Meanwhile, the women from Norway had cruised through the tournament and reached the finals easily. For the American team, years of hard work and sacrifice would come down to a single game against the Norwegian team.

No one expected the Americans to win. After all, just two months earlier, the Norwegians had twice beaten the US squad on American soil. Norway was the heavy favorite.

When the American team took the field at Tianhe Stadium on the evening of November 30, they could hardly believe their eyes. Sixty-five thousand fans had packed the stadium, and the Chinese crowd cheered the American squad like they'd never been cheered before. Chinese fans had enjoyed the Americans' style of play and liked that they were the "Cinderella" story of the tournament, so many had adopted the American team as their own. But the support of the crowd wouldn't be of much help once the game began. The Americans knew that in order to win, they had to play their best game ever.

From the opening whistle, the US team tried to keep possession and attack the Norwegian defense. But the Norwegian squad knew what to expect. They turned the tables and went on the offensive themselves, keeping the ball in the American zone for most of the half.

But the US team made the most of their few opportunities. Despite being double- and triple-teamed, Akers scored on a header to put the Americans ahead 1–0. Norway quickly knotted the score. At halftime, the game was tied.

In the second half, Norway dominated the play. The American squad could do little on offense. It seemed as if it was just a matter of time before Norway would score and win the game.

Yet the US team held on. Mia Hamm raced all over the field, running down the ball and disrupting Norway's passing lanes. Even when Norway did penetrate the Americans' defensive third, one of the American players would make a spectacular play to keep the opponents from scoring.

As the end of the game approached, however, it became obvious that the Americans were running out of steam. The Norwegians played patiently and kept possession. They appeared unconcerned about winning in regulation and seemed to be saving their strength for almost certain overtime.

The American team sensed that, and as the clock ticked down, everyone drew on their final reserve of energy. It was now or never for the American women's soccer team.

Deep in their defensive third, Norway made a halfhearted effort to move downfield before recycling the ball through the back line. With three minutes left on the clock, they made a crucial error. Playing it safe at the eighteen-yard line, Tina Svensson of Norway decided to pass the ball back to goalie Reidun Seth. Seth slowly jogged out to meet the pass.

Michelle Akers sensed what was about to happen. As Svensson turned, bobbled the ball, and made a weak pass back, Akers raced onto the ball, crashing by Svensson and knocking her into a second defender. The Norwegian goalie charged off her line toward the ball. Akers took a touch around the keeper, leaving her alone in front of goal. As Mia had noted, Michelle Akers knew how to keep her composure. From six yards out, she calmly slotted the ball home with her right foot into the untended net.

GOAL!

Michelle's teammates charged the field and swarmed her in celebration. But there were still a few minutes left to play.

In desperation, Norway pushed high up the field, but Mia and the Americans turned back the late surge from Norway.

When the final whistle blew, the United States had won. They were the first Women's World Cup winners ever, going from underdogs to world champions with their win.

For a split second, the whole team stopped as if

they were frozen in place. They just looked at one another in a combination of disbelief and unbridled delight. Then they ran toward one another, laughing and crying and hugging. A few players fell to the ground sobbing with joy. The normally emotionless Coach Dorrance raced from the American bench to join his team on the field.

The Chinese crowd cheered wildly as the bitterly disappointed Norwegian team offered their humbled congratulations. A podium was pulled onto the field, and each player received a gold medal, a huge bouquet of flowers, and the love of fans everywhere. Coach Dorrance was presented with an enormous gold trophy as fireworks shot into the air. With the trophy hoisted above their heads, the US women's national team members were crowned the first world champions.

In an interview, midfielder Julie Foudy spoke for Mia and all their teammates: "When we started the team, we never thought there would be a World Cup. It was always a mystical thing. And now we're holding it."

There was nothing better in the whole world.

CHAPTER SEVEN
1992–1993

BACK TO SCHOOL

Despite all the drama of the inaugural Women's World Cup, the American women's victory caused barely a ripple back in the United States. As far as the American sports media was concerned, women's soccer ranked somewhere below professional wrestling on a scale of importance. Most newspapers didn't even report the win at all. The few that did only mentioned it briefly and barely showed the score.

Yet for the team, the championship meant everything in the world, even if few other Americans recognized their achievement. They knew what they had accomplished together, and that was all they needed. Never before had an American soccer team, male or female, won a world championship. For the American women to do so in the first women's competition ever held was extraordinary. It was the culmination of years of sacrifice and hard work.

But now that the competition was over and the next World Cup not scheduled until 1995, it was time to go back to the real world.

For some of the women, their lives as soccer players were over. They had to find jobs and resume living a normal life. For others, it meant trying to find something to do until the national team reformed in the summer of 1992. For Mia Hamm, it meant going back to school.

Despite the absence of Mia and Coach Dorrance, UNC had still managed to win yet another ACC and NCAA title in 1991.

Mia couldn't wait to return to Chapel Hill. Her time with the national team had been hard work, and she looked forward to living life as a normal college student and athlete. She and several teammates all moved into an off-campus apartment. The group of young women had a great time living together and grew extra close.

When the Tar Heels began practice in the fall of 1992 for the upcoming season, it became obvious to everyone that Mia Hamm was a different player. During her year with the national team, Mia had improved dramatically and had shed the perception that she was a one-dimensional player. In fact, the

World Cup official report had cited her for being one of the best attacking defenders in the tournament. Even Mia admitted that she now had "a much better understanding of what it takes to be a playmaker." When she rejoined the Tar Heels on the field, she demonstrated just how much she had learned.

Installed on the forward line with Kristine Lilly, Mia Hamm had one of the most remarkable seasons of any collegiate athlete in any sport—ever. She dominated that season as no soccer player had ever done before.

Her performance against Duke in the ACC finals epitomized her magnificent season.

Entering the game, Mia led the nation in both goals and assists, and UNC was undefeated. They had won twenty-two straight games that season, but Duke was almost as good. They had lost only four games all year long.

In the first half, Mia helped UNC break through. A little more than sixteen minutes into the match, she lost her defender at the edge of the penalty area just to the right of the goal. In previous seasons, Mia would have tried to take her defender one on one, a strategy that might have resulted in a goal but was more likely to end in a turnover. Now Mia drew on her experience on the national team. She hesitated for a moment, drawing the attention of the defense, and then spotted Lilly open on the left side. She hit her with a pinpoint cross that Lilly volleyed into the back of the net. That put the Tar Heels up by one.

Just moments into the second half, the Duke Blue Devils scored to tie it up at one goal apiece. It was only the second time all season that UNC hadn't led in the second half, and it sucked the air out of the Tar Heels.

As Mia said later, "The last emotion you want to display to your teammates is one of disappointment. It was my job to motivate the other players. There was still a lot of time left."

Mia didn't panic. UNC needed to score, but instead of waiting for the game to come to her, Mia went out and took the game over. Mia decided to run until her lungs burst or her legs fell off. On defense, Mia was a terror. She was everywhere and she cut out the Blue Devils' attack time and time again. With only fifteen minutes remaining, she won another ball and hit Lilly with a spectacular through ball. Lilly passed it first to teammate Rita Tower, who slotted it home to put UNC ahead, 2–1.

UNC could have dropped all ten players and clogged the box to protect the lead, but Mia was on fire. A few minutes later, she spotted Danielle Egan wide open in the penalty area. From an amazing forty-five yards away, Mia put a pinpoint pass on Egan's head. Egan headed the ball in, securing UNC's 3–1 victory and another ACC championship.

Mia hadn't scored a goal, but she had collected three assists and dominated play for all ninety minutes. She was undoubtedly the woman of the match. After the game, Duke coach Bill Hempen was in awe of Mia.

"She's probably the best women's soccer player in the world," he said. "She showed that today."

That may have been the first time anyone had ever said Mia was the best in the world, but it wouldn't be the last.

About a month later, the Tar Heels ended up facing the Duke Blue Devils again in the NCAA finals. Duke had fought its way to the finals, as had UNC. The Blue Devils had been hoping for a rematch and they got their wish, but they would have to beat the best team in the NCAA on their own field—and the Tar Heels didn't lose on their own field. But the Blue Devils refused to be intimidated. They played tough, and seventeen minutes into the game they scored on a header off a corner kick to take an early lead.

Now UNC trailed for just the second time all year. The Tar Heels weren't used to being down and they looked dejected, but their leader never stopped believing. Ten minutes later at the twenty-eight-minute mark, Mia took over the game again, and her performance keyed perhaps the best stretch of soccer any Tar Heels team had ever played.

First Mia lasered in a shot from twelve yards out into the upper ninety on the right side to tie the score. Five minutes later, the Duke defense was so focused on her and Lilly that they allowed Keri Sanchez to deflect in a goal on a corner kick to put UNC ahead 2–1.

Twenty-four seconds later, Mia intercepted a soft pass, turned the ball up the field, beat the defense, and banged in another goal on a counter. Four minutes later, UNC scored again. Before the Blue Devils knew it, they were down 4–1 and reeling. The second half was all North Carolina. Coach Dorrance even benched Mia, but the Tar Heels just kept scoring.

With only eighteen minutes remaining and the Tar Heels up 7–1, Mia pestered Dorrance into putting her back into the game. She wanted to be in the final minutes of the game with senior Kristine Lilly, who was playing her last game for the Tar Heels.

"We don't enjoy embarrassing teams," the coach explained later, "but there's no way I would prevent Mia from playing with the person she admires most."

Mia celebrated with her third and final goal of the match, and UNC won by eight goals and finished the season a perfect 25–0. It was the Tar Heels' seventh consecutive NCAA title. That season North Carolina outscored the opposition by an amazing 132 to 11.

Coach Hempen complimented the Tar Heels in an interview after the match, saying, "They're just awesome, outstanding, unbelievable, anything you can say."

Most observers felt that the 1992 Tar Heels represented the greatest collegiate women's soccer team ever. At the end of the season, Mia won just about every women's soccer award imaginable. She was a unanimous selection as US Soccer Female Athlete of the Year, was named the MVP of both the ACC and NCAA tournaments, led the nation in scoring with a record ninety-two goals, and had thirty-three assists.

That winter Mia trained with the national team again, and in March they went to Cyprus for a three-game series of friendlies against Denmark, Norway, and Germany.

The team learned that as defending World Cup champions, there was now a huge target on their backs. Every other national team was eager to show they could beat the world champions.

Sure enough, after defeating Denmark 2–0, the Americans lost to both Norway and Germany, 1–0. The American victory in the World Cup had served as a wake-up call to women's soccer teams from other nations. Before the Cup, they had assumed that they were better than the United States. But the American win had exposed weaknesses in their soccer programs that they were determined to fix. They proved precisely how hard they were working in the summer of 1993. The US team entered the World University Games as the heavy favorites. But after reaching the finals with little difficulty, they lost to China. With the next World Cup only two years off, the American women knew that in order to repeat as champions they would have to work harder and play a lot better.

Yet as fall approached, Mia Hamm's main priority was for North Carolina to repeat as ACC and NCAA champions. Despite all that the Tar Heels had achieved during her career, she wanted to make sure there was no letdown her senior season.

Without Kristine Lilly, the 1993 Tar Heels weren't quite as potent as they had been the year before, but they were no less effective. Once again, they charged through the regular season with an unblemished record. Even though Mia was now usually double- or triple-teamed, her playmaking ability made it possible for some of her teammates, such as sophomore scoring sensation Tisha Venturini, to pick up the slack.

Still, Mia remained the player UNC looked to when things got rough. Late in the season, the always-tough Duke Blue Devils held Mia scoreless in the first half and looked capable of upsetting the top-ranked Tar Heels. But the second half belonged to Mia. She streaked down the field on the right side and found herself miraculously covered by only a single defender. Her opponent had little chance. Mia stutter-stepped around her as if the player was standing still, then drilled the ball into the narrow gap between the diving goalie and the near post.

Moments later she was at it again. This time she

fought through the crowd to get on the end of a corner kick, which she expertly headed into the net. By the time she scored her third goal, she had all but guaranteed the Tar Heels another ACC championship.

But perhaps the most memorable moment of that season took place off the field. Mia and several of her teammates were sitting around their apartment, which some referred to as "Animal House" due to its constant state of disarray. They were all watching a soccer game when the phone rang. One of Mia's roommates answered it, listened for a moment, and then just started screaming.

One more dream seemed about to be fulfilled. They learned that women's soccer had just been added to the summer Olympic Games, scheduled to be held in Atlanta in 1996, as a full medal sport!

Mia couldn't believe it. "I grew up on the Olympics," she remembered later. "I distinctly remember 1984, cheering all the greats on, like Mary Lou Retton and Jackie Joyner-Kersee. My heroes and idols." The Olympics had a special significance to athletes as an event that many watched and dreamed of participating in. Many of the women's competitions were more popular than the men's. The Olympics was the only competition where the media covered women's sports the way they deserved to be. Every four years, young girls could watch female athletes compete, win, and be treated with the respect they deserved.

Mia said it best: "What an incredible opportunity. You hear all the clichés, that it's a dream come true. Well, it is, for myself and for every young girl growing up who plays any sport."

But before that dream could come true, Mia still had to complete her final collegiate season at UNC. Looking for their eighth straight NCAA title, the Tar Heels met George Mason in the finals at Fetzer Field. Nearly six thousand fans—a record number to see a collegiate women's soccer match—turned out for the game. They all wanted to see Mia put on a show in her final game of college.

Mia's teammates were determined to win. They didn't take any chances.

Only two minutes into the game, Keri Sanchez scored on an unassisted goal to put UNC ahead. Then the Tar Heel defense shut down George Mason and did not allow them a single shot on goal during the entire first half. Meanwhile, UNC scored twice more, including one goal assisted by Mia.

In the second half, with UNC ahead 3–0, Mia stepped to the ball and won it from a George Mason defender. Then she shot past, dribbling the ball and streaking toward the net. The George Mason goalie didn't have a chance. Mia drilled the shot to put UNC ahead 4–0. It would be the last goal of her collegiate career.

With the game in the bag, Coach Dorrance pulled Mia from the game with only a few minutes left. Action on the field stopped as her teammates surrounded her, tears in their eyes, and all 5,721 fans rose to their feet and gave Mia a standing ovation. The noise from the crowd was deafening. It sounded like a crowd two or three times that size.

After the final whistle of the 6–0 UNC win, no one really wanted to talk about how it was North Carolina's eighth straight championship. They just wanted to talk about Mia. She had won four college championships in her four years at UNC. She was a three-time All-American. She won the Missouri Athletic Club (MAC) Player of the Year and the Hermann Trophy as a junior and senior. She had scored 21 or more goals every year at the University of North Carolina, and 103 total over her career.

Add on the 72 career assists, and her 278 career points set the NCAA record for most career points.

"There will never be a player who will break Mia's records," said Coach Dorrance. "They're secure until the end of time. She came here during an incredible era of striking and scoring power."

True to form, Mia didn't have much to say about her accomplishments. She gave credit to her teammates. "The records are not important," she said after the game. "What it shows is the strength of the program and the traditions of the school. It's reflective of the people I'm surrounded with.

"The goals and the championships are nice, but the emotions, the tears, and the smiles on my teammates' faces are my championships."

She didn't know it then, but in the next few years, there would be both smiles and tears for Mia Hamm.

CHAPTER EIGHT
1994–1995

DISAPPOINTMENT

At the end of the season, Mia collected virtually every award and honor possible. Not only did she repeat as national and ACC Player of the Year, but she was also named the Mary Garber Award winner as ACC female Athlete of the Year and was the recipient of the Honda-Broderick Cup, given to the most outstanding female athlete in collegiate sports.

The awards were nice, but after graduating from college, Mia was already looking to the future. The summer of 1994 was a special time for American soccer. For the first time in the history of the World Cup, the men's tournament was going to be staged in the United States. FIFA hoped to spark interest in the sport in the last country that hadn't fallen in love with the beautiful game. The US men's national team were automatically qualified for the World Cup finals for the second World Cup in a row. Before the 1990 World Cup, the men's team hadn't qualified since 1950. Fans from all over the world descended on the United States and turned cities like Palo Alto, California; Los Gatos, California; Dallas, Texas; and Chicago, Illinois, into World Cup parties. The entire country started to catch soccer fever.

Meanwhile, the women's national team was trying to qualify for the next Women's World Cup. If they did, they would get a chance to repeat their title in Sweden in 1995. After that, Mia hoped to compete in the Olympics in 1996.

The hype that surrounded the 1994 World Cup raised the profile of soccer in the United States. That event, coupled with the addition of women's soccer as an Olympic medal event, dramatically changed women's soccer. The national team, which had thus far played and practiced in obscurity, was suddenly the focus of much more attention by the media. Magazines profiled the team's best players. When major corporations realized that the US squad would be favored to win a medal in Atlanta, they were interested in helping to sponsor the national team.

Almost overnight, the women's team began to be treated almost as well as the men's team. Plans were made to create a training center for the team in Florida, and team members were put on salary, which allowed them to focus entirely upon preparing for the World Cup. Mia signed an endorsement contract with Nike, the world's biggest sporting-goods company, which was endorsing the likes of Michael Jordan and Bo Jackson. It was an exciting time to be a female soccer player.

Other nations had the same excited reaction to the news about the Olympics and also started paying more attention to the sport. The upcoming Women's World Cup promised to be much more competitive than the first. The American team wouldn't have an easy time repeating as champions.

As Mia commented to a reporter, "Any one of the teams could beat us this year. We're all basically equal in talent."

In 1994, Coach Dorrance shocked everyone when he announced that he was stepping down as head coach of the national team. Collegiate soccer was expanding rapidly and he felt he could no longer serve as coach of both the national team and UNC. It would be up to new coach Tony DiCicco to direct the team.

The American team had little difficulty in the

qualifying round, defeating all four opponents while giving up only a single goal. Mia played extremely well. Against the team from Trinidad and Tobago, she netted four goals in an 11–1 win.

Yet everything wasn't perfect for the Americans. Michelle Akers was ill with chronic fatigue syndrome and no one was certain how much she would be able to play in the World Cup, or if she would play at all. There were several new members of the team, too. That meant adjustments for everyone, including Mia.

At the same time, Mia's personal life changed. After having dated for several years, she and Christiaan Corry, a Marine pilot, were married on December 17, 1994.

In the year leading up to the World Cup, the team appeared to be just as strong as they had been in 1991. In fourteen friendlies played between the qualifier and the Cup finals, the team lost only once to Denmark and tied Norway. When the final round began, in June 1995, the US team had won its last nine matches. Mia was back playing right wing and appeared right at home. As the team prepared for the Cup, she led the squad by scoring twelve goals in fourteen games. Now just about everyone recognized her as perhaps the greatest player in the game.

Teammate Carin Gabarra, at age thirty, a team veteran, commented that "we've watched her mature into one of the best players in the world." That kind of talk made Mia self-conscious and a little embarrassed.

When someone would ask her if she was the best player in the world, she usually just shook her head and laughed, saying, "I'm not even close." She didn't even think she was the best player on her team. But she was the team's most versatile player, after years of steadily improving every aspect of her game. She was even strong in goal, and listed as the team's third-string goalkeeper for emergency situations.

As she said later, "I worked really hard on my fitness, and I worked really hard on my defensive presence, and what I learned was that I was a lot more confident offensively because of that. I was never tired. A lot of my offensive confidence came from defensive success, winning the ball from a defender and then going forward. I wasn't just thinking, 'Geez, Mia, don't mess up.'"

Coach DiCicco said, "When Mia is on, there's no one better in the world." But during the World Cup,

Mia wasn't on, and neither was the rest of the team. In the opening match of the tournament, on June 6, the United States received a shock. The team was tied by China, 3–3. It had been three years since the US team had given up so many goals in a game.

The tie put the squad in a tough spot. Teams in the finals were divided into multiple groups. In order to reach the knockout round, every team needed to finish either first or second in their group. One more loss could prevent the United States from even reaching the final round.

In their second game, the United States were up 2–0 on Denmark, but with only six minutes remaining in the game, goalkeeper Briana Scurry was ejected on a controversial hand-ball infraction outside the goal box. Since the United States had already used up their three substitutions, Mia had to step into the goal while the United States resumed the game with one less player on the field.

The Danes sensed an opportunity. Apart from winning the Cup outright, defeating the defending champs and knocking them from the finals would be the next best thing. Denmark swarmed the Americans' defensive third, pushing as high up the field as they could. Moments after Mia strapped on the keeper gloves, the Danes were awarded a free kick. Mia hardly knew what to do.

Mia was trying to organize her team into a wall and was still trying to get into position when the Dane took her shot. Fortunately for Mia, it soared over the net. It was a tense moment for the Americans and for Mia. Being a keeper was harder than she thought.

But her ordeal wasn't over. In the final seconds of the game, a Danish player found some space and took a hard shot. This time Mia was in position. She caught the ball against her stomach and a few moments later, the United States escaped with a 2–0 win.

After the game Mia admitted her stint as goalie had left her "scared to death."

"The goal is so much bigger when you're inside it than when you're shooting at it," she said. "I hope I never have to do it again!"

A few days later, the team dispatched Australia 4–1 to win their group, beating out China on a tie-breaker determined by the total number of goals scored. Thus far, Mia had played steady but not spectacular soccer. Her former teammates at UNC,

George Tiedemann / contributor / Getty Images

MIA IN ACTION AS THE US GOALIE

Kristine Lilly and Tisha Venturini, had taken up much of the scoring slack left by Michelle Akers's absence. Defenses focused on Mia, so she found herself back in the role of playmaker. She drew the attention of the defense then passed off to her teammates.

Led by Lilly's two goals, the US team defeated Japan 4–0 in the quarterfinals to reach the semi-finals. The win was a big one for the United States.

Coach DiCicco had gambled and chosen to rest Akers, who was still weak and had also suffered a concussion as well as a knee injury the previous week. In the second half, with the United States leading 3–0, he had rested several other key players, including Mia Hamm. He wanted the team at full strength for their semifinal matchup against Norway.

Since the 1991 Cup finals, the American and Norwegian women's soccer teams had become archrivals. The United States had faced Norway more than any other team in the world except Canada. Many in the media believed they were the two best teams in the world. But in six meetings since the 1991 Cup final, the United States had won only once. Norway always played the Americans tough.

Before the game, Coach DiCicco admitted, "It will be a war. Their players don't like our players. Maybe they're jealous—who knows?" Still, the United States was favored to win.

The Americans knew that they had to play extremely well in order to advance to the next round. The Norwegians played a rough, physical game. From the opening minute of the semifinals, Norway had the Americans on the defensive. Only ten minutes into the game, Norway scored off a corner kick when a header bounced off the crossbar and into the goal. For the rest of the first half, the United States scrambled to find some defensive composure as Norway kept pouring on the pressure.

In the second half, the Americans played better, but just couldn't put the ball into the net. Michelle Akers was playing hurt and got off only one shot the entire game. Although the United States had several good scoring opportunities, they failed to capitalize on them. One goal was all Norway needed. They bounced the Americans from the finals, and the Americans were world champions no more. This time, their tears were not from joy but from sadness, and it was the Americans who offered congratulations to the ecstatic Norwegians.

Michelle Akers summed up her teammates' feelings after the game when she said, "It's like having your guts kicked out of you." Added midfielder Julie Foudy, "It's like someone snatched away our dream."

A few days later, Norway easily defeated Germany to win the World Cup. The United States regrouped and shut out China 2–0 to come in third place. It wasn't a bad finish, but it wasn't what they were hoping for.

The team was determined to improve its performance before the next international competition. In the Olympics, third place means a bronze medal. Mia and her teammates wanted to bring home the gold.

CHAPTER NINE
1996

THE FIRST OLYMPICS

"A lot of times, when I think about doing this," said Mia after the World Cup, "I think to myself, 'Man, I'm really tired.' I've been with this team for eight years. That's a career for a professional football player or basketball player."

Perhaps she had been tired during the World Cup. But if she was, the loss to Norway served to reenergize her and sharpen her resolve. Just a few weeks after the World Cup, Mia couldn't wait to get back together with the team. She had something to prove. When the team regrouped in Orlando in January of 1996, Mia could see a difference in the team's mentality.

As Mia explained later, "We had kind of decided there were certain things we weren't going to do the same way, and there were certain things we were going to do better. Everyone committed themselves to doing that, to being fitter, to being faster, to being stronger, and bringing the team closer together, on the field and off."

The entire team lived together, practiced together, trained together, and even went out together at night. Orlando residents grew accustomed to seeing a large group of extremely fit women making appearances at the city's nightspots.

The team members' dedication to one mutual goal built new bonds and strengthened old ones. This was a tighter group than the one who had played in the World Cup together. The only goal on the women's minds was an Olympic gold medal. No one would be satisfied with anything less.

Mia set the tone for the entire team. As she told one interviewer, "I've worked too hard and too long to let anything stand in the way of my goals. I will not let my team down and I will not let myself down. I'm going to break myself in half to make sure it happens.

"It's in the ninetieth minute that the gold medal will be won," she added, "when we all decide what our comfortable zone is and what our regular role on the team is and push ourselves beyond what we thought we could do. That's what it will take to win the gold."

For the American team, the long road to the Olympics began in Brazil.

After a short training period, in late January they traveled to Brazil and played four friendlies. They won three and tied one. They used the series as a tune-up for a more important challenge just ahead. When they returned to Florida, they had to prepare for a two-game rematch with Norway. Those two games would be a great test for the team. Norway was sure to expose some holes in their game that other teams couldn't. The Norwegians were sure to push the Americans to their edge in the first game and make tactical adjustments for the second.

Even though no title or championship was at stake, the American women knew they would probably have to face the Norwegians in the Olympics, and they needed a win to build their confidence.

In the first game, Mia and the Americans were able to move the ball around more. Mia put the United States ahead with a first-half goal, and the team held on for a 3–2 win. Though they let in two, their three goals scored illustrated the promise of the Americans' attack. But still, the defensive lapse would have to be addressed if they wanted to get to the gold-medal match. In the second game just two days later, Norway had made some adjustments to their defensive scheme that stifled the Americans' ball movement by dropping more defenders behind the ball. With the game tied and only seconds remaining, Norway put one past the Americans to take the game. The Americans would have to wait until the Olympics to get another chance at their biggest rival.

The team used the defeat as extra motivation as they played host to a number of teams in a series of friendlies. Each time they played, they continued to improve.

In March, the team barely avoided a major disaster. Late in a game against Germany, with the United States ahead 1–0, Mia pursued a pass over her head into the German goalkeeper's box. She was running full speed and collided with the goalie as she slid out to gather the ball.

Mia hit the deck hard and lay motionless while her teammates gathered around her. The collision had Mia's head ringing and she was unable to stand up. She had to be stretchered off as players and fans from both nations held their breath in concern.

The US team won the game, 2–0, but they weren't in the mood to celebrate. Everyone was worried about Mia. The team doctor diagnosed the injury as a sprained knee and said Mia would be okay after a few weeks of rest.

Shortly after she returned, she played one of the most amazing games of her career. In a driving rainstorm in Indianapolis, Indiana, she showed the team from France that she really was the best player in the world.

For twenty-three minutes, neither team could score as the soaked field slowed play to a crawl. At the twenty-three-minute mark, Tisha Venturini found Mia in front of the goal. The pass was beautifully weighted. It hit Mia in stride and she rocketed the ball into the net to take a 1–0 lead.

Five minutes later, Mia launched another missile at the French goal. The goalkeeper managed to get her hands on the ball, but deflected it back into play. One of Mia's teammates was in the right place at the right time and knocked it across the goal line to put the United States up by two.

One minute later, it was 3–0 after Mia tracked down a loose ball and put it past the French goalie. The United States scored again to go up 4–0, then Mia made yet another goal. Two minutes after that, she assisted on a goal by Michelle Akers and increased the Americans' lead to 6–0. In the second half, she scored again, and the United States would go on to beat the French 8–2. Mia had scored four goals and assisted on two others! Everyone was blown away by her performance. It was one of the greatest performances in the history of women's soccer and forced many doubters to reconsider their opinion of women playing soccer. Mia was masterful in every facet of the game.

By the time the Olympics began in late July, the US women's soccer team was on a roll. They hadn't lost a game since the defeat by Norway five months earlier. And now they were firing on all cylinders.

Much like the World Cup, the Olympic soccer competition began with group play. To make it to the medal round, the Americans first had to finish as one of the top two teams in their group.

They played their first match on July 21 against Denmark. Although the Olympics were based in Atlanta, Georgia, Olympic soccer games were held in several different cities across the United States. The first game was played in Orlando, Florida, where the Americans trained. It was like playing in their backyard. Tiffeny Milbrett, Julie Foudy,

Michelle Akers, Kristine Lilly, and Mia Hamm were about as comfortable as they could get. The United States was paired with China, Sweden, and Denmark in Group E. It was a tough group and it would take three stellar games to move on to the knockout round.

Twenty-five thousand fans—at the time, the most ever to watch a women's soccer game in the United States—turned out for the first match under the blazing Florida sun. The temperature on the field was more than 100 degrees Fahrenheit. Yet Mia Hamm sent everyone home happy. Everyone except the Danes, that is.

Mia was all over the field, hounding the ball on defense and commanding the American attack. While everyone else was gasping for air, Mia ran around as if she had an extra lung.

With the United States ahead 1–0, Mia took a header from Akers and put on a patented burst of speed that left her defender trailing behind, struggling to catch up. Mia took a few touches inside the penalty box and ripped a high and hard shot that hit the left corner. It all happened so fast that most of the people in the crowd missed it.

Four minutes into the second half, she did it

again. She got the ball on the right side of the penalty area and found her lane to the goal blocked by two defenders, so she faked right, pushed left, then forward, and pulled the ball back. Two Danish defenders stumbled and lost their balance with the change of direction. She burst by them and slotted a short pass to teammate Tiffeny Milbrett, who kicked it into the net. The United States won 3–0.

Mia's performance stunned soccer fans and media from around the world. They were accustomed to seeing such play from men—from players like the great Pelé or Argentine star Diego Maradona. But they were shocked to discover that a woman could play with the same combination of speed, strength, and grace. With the world watching, Mia had made a statement that soccer doesn't care if you are male or female, it only cares how you play the game.

"Every time she got the ball she was dangerous," explained Coach DiCicco after the game. "She was the key player for us. Mia took the game over."

Danish coach Keld Gantzhorn concurred. "We made a little mistake, and she said, 'Thank you' and scored. I am sure we saw one of the best teams in competition," he added. "I am sure they will reach the final."

During the Olympic group stage, games were played at a breakneck pace. With a game every few days, it is very hard to play at a consistently high level. Soccer players run about ten miles per game and exert a lot of physical and mental energy. It takes time to recover, but during the Olympics they didn't have that luxury. The Americans had to play their next games just two days later.

That game demonstrated just how difficult it is to win an Olympic medal, let alone a gold. The Swedes had seen Mia's performance against Denmark, and they were determined not to let her beat them. She was double-teamed most of the game. On at least seven different occasions she was knocked to the ground. The final time, following a collision with the Swedish goalkeeper, Mia crawled from the field on her hands and knees with a badly sprained left ankle.

Although the United States defeated Sweden 2–1, the player the team could least afford to lose was hurt and had little time to recover. Following the game, Coach DiCicco announced that Mia's playing status was "day-to-day."

The team traveled to Miami to face China, a team that had become one of their fiercest rivals over the last few years. With either a win or tie, each team could qualify for the medal round.

The game against China might have been the hardest game for Mia during that tournament. After appearing in more than one hundred consecutive international matches for the American team, Mia couldn't play. Her ankle was so sore that she could barely walk. Coach DiCicco had included Mia as a possible substitute, but it seemed unlikely that he would risk his best player's ability to play in the entire tournament for the sake of one game. Mia would have to watch the game from the bench.

Her teammates didn't let her down. With Mia out of the lineup, China decided to play a conservative and defensive game. The Americans dominated play and outshot China by more than a two-to-one margin but couldn't score.

Neither could the Chinese. And in the end, both teams advanced to the knockout round, but China won the group on goal differential.

After their first-game tie with Brazil, gold-medal favorite Norway had recovered to win twice and also advance along with a surprisingly strong Brazilian team. The US team had to face Norway in the semifinal matchup, and China would play Brazil. If the United States won, they would play the winner of the China-Brazil match for the gold medal. If the Americans lost, their Olympic run would be over.

Before the game, Mia had her ankle heavily taped. It was still sore and hurt to run on, but she felt she could play. Coach DiCicco trusted his star player to tell him the truth and he put her back in the starting lineup. He knew that even if she wasn't quite at 100 percent, Norway would still have to pay attention to her, and that might open up a goal-scoring opportunity for other players.

As always, the Norwegians played the Americans tough and physical. They focused on defense and, taking a lesson from the Swedes, decided to play Mia close. They knew she wasn't playing at 100 percent, and Norway's players sent Mia tumbling to the ground time after time. Her teammates' pleas for a penalty were not heard by the referee, who let the Norwegians continue to play.

Nearly sixty-five thousand fans turned up to watch the USA take on Norway that day, almost all of them rooting for the Americans. Only eighteen minutes into the game, Norway took advantage of a rare lapse by the consistently strong American defense. A Norwegian player got free on a breakaway and scored to put Norway ahead 1–0. It felt like the World Cup semifinal all over again, but this time the difference was the Americans' mentality. That goal didn't shake their resolve one bit—they knew they could outplay Norway.

"We had done the exact same thing the summer prior in 1995 and lost. That was in the World Cup semifinal," remembered midfielder Julie Foudy years after the Olympic game. "This time around, instead of panic, it's like we're fine. There was calmness to that group. There was a feeling that we're not going to let this slip out of our hands."

The lead held through the first half. Although the Americans were dominating play, they just couldn't score. Then with only twelve minutes to play, Mia got the ball in the penalty area and the crowd leaped to their feet. Several Norwegian players closed on her once more and knocked her viciously to the ground, stripping her of the ball. It looked as if the United States had just lost another scoring opportunity. The crowd groaned. But this time the referee blew the whistle and stopped play. At long last, the official finally called a penalty on one of Mia's takedowns. The Americans would receive a penalty kick!

On another day, Coach DiCicco may have allowed Mia to take the kick herself. But he knew her ankle was sore, and besides, Michelle Akers still had the most powerful shot in all of women's soccer.

The ball was placed on the ground twelve yards from the goal. Players from both teams stood back and watched as Akers set up behind the ball. The Norwegian goalkeeper crouched, slowly rocking from one side to the other, trying to stay loose. The crowd fell silent.

Then Akers took off toward the ball. The goalie dove, trying to anticipate her shot.

Boom! The kick ripped into the back of the net.

Goal! The game was tied.

Twelve minutes later, it ended. But in the final round, there are no ties. The game entered overtime.

The US team would not be denied the opportunity to play for the gold medal. Only ten minutes into overtime, Foudy made a ten-yard run on the ball before threading a perfect pass to Shannon MacMillan. On the American team's twenty-eighth shot of the game, the ball finally made it past the goalkeeper from the run of play. The United States won 2–1! Despite her sprained ankle, Mia Hamm had played every minute of the game.

Now it was time to go for the gold.

China had easily defeated Brazil in the other semifinal to set up a rematch with the United States on August 1, 1996, for the gold medal. Although the Americans were heavy favorites, the team was determined not to take the Chinese team lightly.

"China is a very good team," warned Coach DiCicco. "In the group match, they played for a tie. We can't expect that in the final."

The Americans would see a very different style of play from China in the final, but the Americans would have Mia, whom they had sorely missed the last time these two teams met.

Nothing prepared the American team for the reception they received when they stepped out onto the field at Sanford Stadium. The huge arena was filled to capacity with more than seventy-six thousand fans, most chanting "USA! USA!" over and over. That year women's soccer broke the record for highest attendance multiple times, but the gold-medal game shattered the previous record.

Everyone on the team, including Mia Hamm, couldn't help but think back to the long practices and scrimmages they had played with no one watching at all, or the dozens of games they had played before only a few hundred fans, or to a time when the United States didn't even have a women's team. Their own effort and determination had helped turn women's soccer into a sport that people cared about. Each day, Mia received hundreds of fan letters from young soccer players. It was almost impossible for any of the women to walk around in public. Everywhere they went, fans mobbed them.

When Mia looked up into the crowd, she knew her parents and the rest of her family were all watching. She wanted to make them proud, particularly her brother Garrett. His illness had slowly grown worse. He even had to quit his job to focus all his energies on his health. Although Mia had pulled a groin muscle in practice the previous day, adding to the discomfort already caused by her sore ankle, her injuries were nothing compared to what he had been going through. She wanted to represent her family and her country on the field—she wanted to make them proud.

As soon as Mia and her teammates started warming up, they stopped hearing the crowd. They were on the field for one reason and one reason only—to win the gold medal.

When the game began, the Americans soon learned

that Coach DiCicco had been right. The Chinese were playing much more aggressively. In the first few minutes of the game, most of the action took place at midfield as each team probed the other, looking for an opening.

Nineteen minutes into the game, Kristine Lilly carried the ball deep down the left flank. Without even thinking, Mia started her run to the center of the box. The two women had played together for so long that each knew exactly what the other was going to do, and Mia instinctively knew where Kristine would try to put the ball. Kristine pumped a deep cross to the back post right as Mia made a late run. Mia timed her run perfectly and none of the Chinese defenders were able to pick her up.

Boom! She kicked the ball toward the goal, low to the ground.

The crowd started to roar, then stopped and began to groan as they saw the Chinese goalkeeper dive toward the ball and partially block it with her hand. The ball ricocheted to the side, struck the post, and bounced back into play. The trailing Shannon MacMillan pounced on the rebound and hit the ball with her left foot past the keeper.

Shannon sprinted back toward the center circle

David E. Klutho / contributor / Getty Images

MIA AIMS FOR THE GOAL DURING THE 1996 OLYMPIC GOLD MEDAL GAME.

and dove headfirst onto the grass. She slid to a stop as her teammates slid in to meet her. The crowd was cheering again, louder and longer than any of the American women had ever heard a crowd cheer before. The United States led China 1–0.

But the Chinese didn't give up. They weathered another American attack a few minutes later, then slowly regained control of play. At the twenty-nine-minute mark, US goalie Briana Scurry charged off her line to meet Sun Wen of China, who chipped a soft shot just over Scurry's arms and into the net to tie the game. At halftime, the score was even at 1–1.

The Americans tried to catch their breath during halftime, and Coach DiCicco moved from player to player offering words of encouragement. Mia was feeling uncertain about her ability to help the team. Her ankle throbbed so much that she could barely think, and she felt a sharp pain in her groin every time she ran at full speed. She was afraid she was hurting her team with her poor play. Perhaps, she thought, it would be better if she sat out the second half.

She turned to teammate Shannon MacMillan and said, "I'm not able to run very well. Am I hurting the team? Should I take myself out?"

MacMillan looked at Mia as if she had just stepped off an alien spacecraft.

"Are you kidding?!" she blurted out. "We need you. Even if you're not one hundred percent, the Chinese have to worry about you, which means someone else might get free."

Unconvinced, Mia asked several other teammates for their opinion. The vote was unanimous. Everyone thought Mia should keep playing.

In the second half, Shannon MacMillan's take

on Mia's impact on the game proved to be correct. Time after time, she led the American attack on the Chinese goal, only to be stopped by some brilliant work by the Chinese goalkeeper.

With twenty-two minutes remaining, a ball squirted toward Mia on the right touchline off a strong challenge from a Chinese defender. She turned to play the ball and two defenders closed her down. With her first touch, she slipped a perfect ball around the last defender as Joy Fawcett made a deep overlapping run. Joy picked up her head to see Tiffeny Milbrett slip her defender in front of the net. Fawcett crossed the ball to Milbrett, who expertly kicked the ball past the Chinese goalie.

Score! The United States led 2–1. A gold medal was only twenty-two minutes away.

For most of the American team, those twenty-two minutes seemed to take forever. China played as hard as they could, but the American defense just wouldn't break down. The more players the Chinese pushed forward, the tighter the Americans' defense got.

Mia continued chasing down loose balls and covering her mark until her ankle simply gave out. She fell to the ground and couldn't continue. She had given everything she had. As she had promised months before, she had pushed herself beyond what she thought she could do. She was carried from the field to the thunderous cheers of her fans.

Mia hadn't let her teammates down, and they wouldn't let her down, either. The last sixty seconds of the game felt like an eternity to the United States. They had possession of the ball and were desperately trying to run out the remaining time while China was desperately trying to regain possession and tie up the game. Finally, the whistle blew and the game was over. The US women's soccer team had won the first-ever women's Olympic soccer gold medal!

From out of nowhere, star-spangled flags were handed to the American players, who wrapped the flags around their shoulders and lifted them into the air before running around the field, cheering and waving to the crowd. As much as she wanted to, Mia couldn't join them. Her ankle was useless. She limped out to the middle of the field with a wide smile on her face. Two of the team's trainers, and then her teammates, helped her join the team's victory lap to the gold-medal ceremony. "The Star-Spangled Banner" was played over the speakers, the

American flag was raised, and every member of the team stared at the flag with tears in her eyes.

It had taken a tremendous amount of work, but at that moment, no one on the team had any doubt that it had been worth it. They had completely forgotten all the pain, suffering, and sacrifice the minute the Olympic gold medals were placed around their necks.

Mia didn't score or fill up a stat sheet, but her performance on a bum ankle was the difference maker that game. Afterward, the media crowded around Mia. They had correctly anointed her as the team's hero of the moment.

But as they pressed her to comment about her performance, Mia did what she always did: she gave all the credit to her teammates.

"This team is incredible," she told them. "We all believed in each other and we believed in this day. From the beginning, this has been an entire team effort."

It was up to Mia's teammates to speak up for her. "Mia impacts the game whether she scores or not," said Brandi Chastain. "She tears defenses apart. She is awesome."

Tisha Venturini added, "Mia was incredible. I

don't know how she kept going. She's something special."

For Mia, the most gratifying moment of the Olympic Games came when the team returned to their hotel after the big victory. As Mia gingerly stepped from the team van, she spotted her brother Garrett.

Despite being seriously ill, he had watched the game, and now he pushed through the crowd waiting to greet the team to put his arms around Mia. With tears streaming down his face, he whispered, "I'm so proud of you."

As Mia later admitted to a reporter, "That meant so much to me. It wouldn't have been complete without having Garrett there."

After that, the gold medalists did some serious celebrating. After all, they'd earned it.

CHAPTER TEN
1996–1999

MOVING AHEAD

Although Mia had looked forward to taking a vacation with her husband after the Olympics, she discovered she had precious little time to do so. After winning the gold medal, the women's team in general and Mia in particular were in high demand. Mia was more popular and beloved than ever, and there was no denying that she was now a big star.

At least that's what others thought. As far as Mia was concerned, she was the same person she'd always been. It seemed as if every magazine in the country wanted to interview her, and most asked the same question: "How does it feel to be the best women's soccer player in the world?"

Invariably Mia would just shake her head. "I'm not," she would insist over and over. Her protestations did little good. The American public had fallen in love with Mia Hamm.

Young girls considered her a hero, a notion Mia

scoffed at. Yet she still felt responsible for setting a good example. When she made public appearances at soccer clinics or schools, she was always mobbed by groups of girls screaming her name and asking for her autograph. She signed as many as she could. She knew that for kids, meeting someone they considered a hero would make an impression. She wanted to make sure it was a positive one.

Mia's fame reached beyond young athletes who played or watched soccer. Corporate America discovered her and in the wake of the Olympics considered her to be the perfect spokeswoman. She did television and magazine endorsements for a variety of products, such as shampoo, sports equipment, soda, and nutritional sports bars.

After so many years of playing soccer for no salary, Mia was happy to be more financially successful. But all the publicity made her a little uncomfortable.

"It's weird getting attention," she said. "I'm not this perfect person," she kept insisting.

She knew there was much more to life than winning gold medals and being famous. Garrett had taught her that.

When she signed autographs and spoke before

groups, she often handed out copies of a small flyer. It described the disease that afflicted her brother, aplastic anemia, and urged people to have a simple blood test done for bone marrow screening. If someone with healthy bone marrow is a match for someone with aplastic anemia and certain other illnesses, a bone marrow transplant can help the sick person survive. In Garrett's case, the situation was particularly dire and doctors feared he would die if he didn't get a transplant soon. In most instances, family members can be donors, but since Garrett was adopted, no one in Mia's family was a match.

After years of waiting for a transplant, an appropriate donor was finally located in February 1997.

At first, it appeared that the operation was a success, as Garrett began to feel like his old self. But he soon got sick again. He contracted a fungal infection. After being ill for so long, his body was too weak to fight it off. In April 1997, Garrett died.

Mia was devastated. "I've been blessed by so many things," she said later on, "but I would give them all up to have him back."

Mia knew that the last thing Garrett would have wanted was for her to stop reaching for her dreams. She was still a member of the national team and turned to her teammates for support. When the Americans played in the Nike US Women's Cup, every member of the team wore a black armband in Garrett's memory. The United States won the Cup and Mia was named MVP.

But while her teammates helped Mia get through a difficult time, they also made certain that she didn't allow her sudden fame to go to her head. When *People* magazine selected her as one of the fifty most beautiful people in the world in May 1997, her teammates teased her constantly.

Yet at the same time, they were also proud. As teammate Julie Foudy said, "Mia has natural beauty. It's not something she has to spend a thousand dollars on."

They appreciated that the team was in some way responsible for making people realize that it was okay for a woman to be an athlete and for helping young girls to see that it was possible to play sports and be admired. They needn't have worried about Mia getting a big head. No matter how much attention she got, she still considered herself a soccer player first.

Even beyond her fame, 1997 marked a year of possibilities for Mia. She had been named US Soccer's Female Athlete of the Year for 1996 for the third consecutive year, and now she was closing in on two important milestones: one hundred career goals and the world record for career goals.

But to Mia, reaching those personal goals took a backseat to helping the team win.

In October of 1997 in Chicago, the team learned that maintaining the level of play that they had enjoyed during their Olympic run was harder than they would have imagined. The German team crushed the US team 3–0. It was the Americans' first defeat in thirty-one matches.

The team was embarrassed by the defeat, but had little time to dwell on the loss. Immediately after the game, they flew to Germany for a rematch. The confident Germans opened the game fired up, and had two scoring chances in the first five minutes. Then the Americans slowly took control. In the thirty-first minute, Tiffeny Milbrett sent a delicate pass to Mia, who cut to the ball at the top of the penalty box. As the defender charged, Mia deftly sidestepped around her, took one touch, and rolled the ball into the net with her left foot to put the United States ahead 1–0.

Five minutes later Tisha Venturini scored to

increase the lead to 2–0. And late in the game Mia added a second goal on a header off a long cross by Shannon MacMillan. The Americans won 3–0. It was an important victory because the team proved to themselves that they were still strong, but they also were feeling the pressure—it takes a lot of energy to be the best.

The Americans ended the 1997 season on a low note, losing to Brazil 1–0. With the important Guangzhou Tournament in China on the horizon, the defending Olympic champions knew they had to start playing better.

That's just what they did. In China, they defeated Sweden and tied the host team to make it to the final against archrival Norway. They hadn't forgotten how they felt when they lost to Norway in the 1995 World Cup semifinals and were glad to have the chance at another rematch.

With the United States ahead 1–0, Mia broke free late in the first half. She dribbled nearly forty yards downfield before unleashing a shot. But goalkeeper Bente Nordby made a spectacular save.

Mia didn't let the near miss slow her down. Just after the beginning of the second half, she slipped a pass in behind the Norwegian defense to free

Kristine Lilly. When Lilly saw that the goalie had committed herself, she passed the ball back to Mia. Mia nailed a left-footed shot into the right corner. The United States went on to win 3–0 and Mia was named tournament MVP.

The team was playing well. If they kept on track, they could be unstoppable. But in a 2–1 victory over Japan in May, Mia pulled her right hamstring. In the same game, Tiffeny Milbrett strained a tendon in her foot.

Milbrett healed quickly, but Mia missed several games. She returned to action on June 25, 1998, in St. Louis for a match with Germany. The Germans were still a strong team and getting stronger all the time. Some observers were already calling them the favorites to win the upcoming World Cup.

The Germans took a 1–0 lead. On defense, they focused on Mia. Each time she touched the ball, she was marked aggressively. Finally, in the fifty-sixth minute, German defender Steffi Jones received a yellow card after needlessly knocking Mia to the ground.

A few minutes later, Coach DiCicco pulled Mia from the game. Her hamstring had held up well, but he didn't want her to push it and get hurt.

Fortunately, Cindy Parlow scored a few minutes later and the United States emerged with a 1–1 tie.

Three days later, the two teams played a rematch. Mia was determined not to allow the Germans to intimidate her.

The Americans went into halftime up a goal. Moments into the second half, Steffi Jones tried to clear the ball from the German end, but inadvertently stepped on the ball and fell down.

Now Mia got her revenge. She collected the ball, went straight at the goal, and rolled a low shot past the keeper.

Two minutes later, she struck again. Julie Foudy stole a pass and fed Mia on the right side of the penalty box. Mia froze a German defender, then stuck a shot into the left corner to put the United States ahead 3–0.

The Germans scored a goal soon after, but it wasn't nearly enough. With the score 3–1, Tiffeny Milbrett shed a defender and sent a perfect cross into the penalty area. Mia fought her way to the ball and volleyed it into the top of the net for a hat trick and her ninety-second international goal. Though the Germans managed to score once more, the day belonged to the Americans to the tune of 4–2.

TIM SLOAN / staff / Getty Images

MIA PLAYING AGAINST GERMANY

One month later, the team began competition in the Goodwill Games, played in the United States. The four teams in the tournament—Denmark, China, Norway, and the United States—were all among the best in the world at that time.

In the opening match, the United States played Denmark. The Danes held the Americans shotless for eighteen minutes, but then Mia and her team-mates exploded. Mia took a pass from Kristine Lilly, then split the defenders. Lilly converted from ten yards to give the Americans a one-goal advantage. Michelle Akers added another goal a few minutes later.

The second half was Mia's time. With the help of her teammates and some expertly run offense, she scored a hat trick in her second consecutive game, giving her ninety-five career goals in 151 games and helping the Americans to a 5–0 drubbing of Denmark.

The victory earned the Americans a spot in the finals against China, who had defeated Norway in the other semifinal.

Before the game Coach DiCicco told his team, "This is important with the World Cup being [in the United States] next year. We don't want China, or any other team, to feel they can beat us here."

From the very beginning, the game was close. Of all the other teams in the world, China was perhaps the only one that could match the Americans' athleticism, speed, discipline, and intensity.

In the first half, neither team was able to score. Mia was repeatedly hammered by the physical Chinese defense. Once, she crumpled to the ground when she was sandwiched by two Chinese defenders. Fortunately, she wasn't hurt.

In the sixty-sixth minute, the Americans finally found a seam in the Chinese defense. As the Chinese defense collapsed around Kristine Lilly on the right side, she passed the ball across to Mia. Mia gave it a quick touch, then spun it into the left side of the net.

"I hit it as hard as I could," she said later. "Thank goodness it went in."

The goal hurt the Chinese team's confidence. Twenty minutes later, Mia collected a free ball, spun, and sent in a booming shot from thirty-five yards out. As soon as she scored, Mia ran the length of the field to the American bench, then slid on her knees in celebration before her cheering teammates.

"Mia turned in a Michael Jordan–like performance tonight," said Coach DiCicco after the 2–0 win.

"I thought before the game that she was the best player in the world," admitted Chinese player Zhao Yan after the game. "And I still feel that way."

After winning the gold medal in the Goodwill Games, Mia continued her assault on the record book. In the opening match of the Nike US Women's

Cup in September 1998, she scored twice against Mexico for her ninety-eighth and ninety-ninth career goals. She also collected a remarkable four assists as the United States ran away with a 9–0 win.

In her next game, against Russia before thirteen thousand fans in Rochester, New York, Mia ran down a bouncing ball and ripped a volley high into the left side of the net for her one hundredth goal. The game was stopped for several minutes as her teammates surrounded her and captain Carla Overbeck presented her with the ball.

"It was a fantastic night, certainly one that I will remember forever," she said. "The crowd was great and it was a lot of fun, but it was even better because I could share it with my teammates. It's a credit to this team that we can have moments like this."

She proved yet again that the team was more important to her than personal glory in the finals against Brazil. Mia didn't score a goal, but rather collected two assists as the United States scored three goals and shut out Brazil for another trophy.

After the win, the team took some much-needed time off. This was also a time that Mia looked for a new way to help others, and the Mia Hamm Foundation was created in 1999. The nonprofit national organization was dedicated to two of the issues most important to Mia: raising money and awareness for those who need bone marrow transplants, and developing opportunities for young women in sports. The Mia Hamm Foundation's mission is a beautiful tribute to Mia's brother Garrett and to Mia's legacy.

When Mia and her teammates gathered together again, it would be to begin final preparations for their real goal, the only one that now mattered to the national team.

They all wanted a chance at another World Cup championship.

CHAPTER ELEVEN 1999

RETURN TO THE CUP

To prepare for the World Cup, the team went to training camp together in December. Coach DiCicco needed time to make his final roster decisions. Then the team embarked on an ambitious exhibition schedule to prepare for Cup competition and drum up public interest in the games.

Wherever the team went, Mia was the focus of the attention. By far, she was the most famous women's soccer player in the world. For many Americans, Mia was the only soccer player they knew by name or could recognize. Wherever she went, she was mobbed by young fans, and there was an intense pressure to play up to her usual high standard. She didn't disappoint. Mia and her teammates were also aware that the record for most goals scored was well within reach.

Italian footballer Elisabetta "Betty" Vignotto had reportedly scored 107 goals in 109 appearances.

Betty had played from 1970 to 1990 in Italy and was a key member of Italy's national team for almost twenty years. During those years, the records of games were not always saved or recorded well, so no one could prove the exact number of goals Betty had scored. But she claimed 107 goals and that became the number to beat. Now Mia was getting close to the total and she kept trying to ignore it.

Mia tallied goal number 103 in the first match of the season against Portugal in a 7–0 win, and notched number 104 three days later in a rematch with Portugal in another US win. One month later, she scored number 105 against Finland.

But when the United States team traveled to Portugal for the Algarve Cup, a tournament with the best European teams as well as China and Australia, Mia went into a slump. Although the American team won the tournament, she didn't score a single goal. With all the attention, Mia wanted to get it over with. The pressure was immense. On one level, Mia really didn't care. As long as her team was winning, she was happy. But on another level, she was concerned. Her teammates depended on her to score. She didn't want to let them down, and she didn't want to lose confidence before entering the World Cup.

Finally, on May 2 in Atlanta, Mia broke out of her slump by curling a twenty-yard blast around the Japanese goalkeeper. It was goal number 106 of her international career.

"I always want to score goals," she said later, "but the important thing is that we win. If I'm not putting the ball into the net, someone will step up to get the job done."

In the end, it was Mia who got the job done. On May 22 against the tough Brazil squad, she scored record-setting goal number 108. It was a fabulous one. Mia started to counter, then passed to Kristine Lilly, who found Cindy Parlow. Parlow put Mia in on goal and Mia finished it.

"I saw her out there [on the wing], got her the ball, and just watched her work the magic," Parlow said.

It was a magical goal, but Mia wanted to share it with her teammates rather than boast about it.

"It was special to get the record on such a great team goal," Mia said after the game.

With the pressure to break the record out of the way, Mia could now focus on helping her team win the World Cup.

Interest in the World Cup continued to grow. One of the reasons was a series of commercials featuring members of the team. One showed Mia playing a variety of sports against Michael Jordan.

Mia laughed when reporters asked her if she was actually able to keep up with Jordan, saying, "I have so much respect for him—you watch him play and you're speechless." Regardless, the commercial made the point that Mia was just as much an athlete as Jordan.

It was obvious that Mia had struck a positive chord when the team took the field on June 19, 1999, at the Meadowlands in New Jersey for the opening game of the World Cup against Denmark. The stadium was packed to capacity with more than seventy-eight thousand fans. Hundreds, maybe thousands of young soccer players, both male and female, wore replicas of Mia's signature number nine jersey. It was Mia-mania! The crowd started cheering at the beginning of the match and kept it up the whole game.

Mia and her teammates didn't let them down. After a slow start with players on both teams fighting early-game jitters, the United States struck first.

Mia broke downfield, outrunning several defenders who simply didn't have enough speed to keep up with her. Brandi Chastain switched the attack with a cross to the far side of the field. Mia took the pass out of the air, dropped it to her feet, and cut it left around the defender. The defender barely got a toe on the ball, but caused it to pop off the grass, and Mia chested the ball to regain control before smashing a left-footed side volley into the top netting. It was the first goal of the 1999 Women's World Cup.

The Danes couldn't keep up with her after that. For the rest of the match, Mia ran them ragged. But as the game entered its final twenty minutes, the United States still led just 1–0. They needed another goal to put the game away.

In the seventy-second minute, Mia threw the ball in from the right side. She followed the ball, and her teammate gave it back to her on a "give and go." Mia took control at the side of the penalty box. She was cut off from the goal, but she spotted teammate Julie Foudy streaking down the opposite side. Her long cross pass hit Foudy in midstride. Foudy knocked the ball into the goal off the near post. A few moments later, they scored again and the United States comfortably won the match 3–0. They also put every team in the World Cup on notice: they were serious about winning another championship.

After the game, everyone was talking about Mia.

"Mia was awesome," Coach DiCicco said simply. Team co-captain Julie Foudy agreed. "When she made that first goal," she said, "I think we were all like, 'Yeah, we're going to be okay.'"

Mia, of course, downplayed her role. "To tell the truth," she said afterward, "I don't remember it, but I was excited." Then, when a reporter asked her about the crowd and all the young players wearing her jersey, Mia lit up. "I feel good about that," she said. "When they leave the stadium, they want to play in the World Cup. That's what it was about."

In their next match, the United States faced Nigeria, a quick, athletic team they knew little about. More than sixty thousand fans showed up to Chicago's Soldier Field and were buzzing to see the Americans win another game. But just two minutes into the match, the Nigerians scored and the crowd went silent. The favored Americans didn't intimidate the Nigerian team. For the next seventeen minutes, the inspired Nigerians played the Americans, and Mia in particular, very close.

Mia knew something needed to be done, so she

took the game over with her speed and footwork. From the left sideline, she rocketed a kick off defender Ifeanyichukwu Chiejine. Michelle Akers dove toward the free ball and got her foot on it, deflecting it into the net to tie the game.

Less than a minute later, Mia struck again. She was left alone on the right wing and Kristine Lilly hit her on a streaking run. Goalkeeper Ann Chiejine was out of position. But when she saw Mia, the keeper started frantically backpedaling toward the goal. Too late. Mia chipped a rocket that sailed over Chiejine's head and into the net to make the score 2–1.

Once the young Nigerian team fell behind, they panicked and lost their composure. They never recovered after the second goal. The Americans rolled to a convincing 7–1 win. In their final game of group play, the United States beat North Korea to make it to the final round. They were only three wins away from winning the World Cup.

The group stage had been a success for the Americans and for the tournament. The average attendance of every match was almost thirty thousand fans. That was way more than had attended in 1995 in Sweden. It was an exciting time to be a part of soccer.

After winning their group, the US team had drawn the tough Germans in the quarterfinals. From the beginning of the match, the Germans made it clear that they intended to do everything they could to stop Mia, including marking her as physically as the referee would allow.

When the United States allowed an own goal only five minutes into the match as Brandi Chastain booted the ball past goalie Briana Scurry, it was a gut check for the whole team. They could have gotten down on Brandi or started to fall apart, but they battled back instead. Though the United States managed to score a goal, the Germans kept the pressure on and scored again just before halftime to take a 2–1 lead into the break.

During halftime the Americans calmed themselves and regrouped. They had been down before. They had dealt with tough, physical opponents before. They knew that there was a whole half left to play and they could get back in the game.

Four minutes into the second half, the United States earned a corner kick. Mia placed the ball on the ground and prepared to kick, surveying the players grouped before the goal. She paused for a moment to gather herself, then hit a curling cross in front of the goal. Brandi Chastain made up for her earlier error by fighting her way through the crowd and sending a header into the net to tie the game.

With that goal, the whole stadium could feel the momentum shift from the Germans to the United States. Twenty-one minutes later, the United States scored the game-winner when Joy Fawcett headed in another goal off a corner from Shannon MacMillan. The Americans' strong second-half defensive effort and some strong set pieces had made the difference. With their 3–2 win, the United States advanced to the semifinals.

Only Brazil stood in their way of reaching the final game. The teams met on the Fourth of July at Stanford University in Palo Alto, California, before another at-capacity crowd. Like the Nigerians, whom Brazil had beaten to reach the final round, the Brazilians were a quick, athletic team. And like the Nigerians, they weren't intimidated. Brazil had long been one of the best soccer countries in the world. Many of the greatest players had come from Brazil. And over the last ten years, the Brazilian women's team was becoming one of the most technical and gifted teams in the world. That team had thirty-two-year-old midfielder Sissi, who was on fire. She was taking the tournament by storm.

The US team may have been looking ahead to the final rather than completely focusing on the game they were playing, or maybe they were just having an off day; who knows? Whatever the cause, they definitely struggled to keep Sissi and the Brazilians away from the goal. All game long the Brazilians put shots on goal. Low and hard shots, corner-kick killers, shots to the upper ninety, but American keeper Briana Scurry was a brick wall that game. She got a hand, foot, or head on every shot that came her way. She smothered loose balls in front of the net and she knew exactly when to leave her line and when to be patient. She was simply outstanding. She shut out the Brazilians despite their many excellent shots, allowing the Americans to win the game 2–0.

Briana's performance sent the Americans into a finals matchup with their rivals. China had defeated Norway by a convincing score of 5–0 in the other semifinal. Both teams had a week to prepare for the final and to get healthy.

Mia needed the time to recharge. Although she hadn't scored since the second game of the tournament, she'd been the focus of every defense that the Americans had faced. Opposing teams had figured out that without Mia, the Americans were a much easier team to play. They sent their toughest defenders to play Mia as physically as possible to either eliminate Mia's touches on the ball or to wear her down. It worked. Mia was exhausted, battered, and bruised. She needed that week to get back to full strength so that she could play well in the finals.

On the Chinese team, Sun Wen was playing some of the best soccer of her career. She was to China what Mia Hamm was to the United States. Both were amazing players in the peaks of their careers. Sun Wen had already scored seven goals in the tournament.

"When we're gonna go against the Chinese we make sure that we always stop Sun Wen," said Tiffeny Milbrett. "If we can stop her we can probably stop China."

Everyone in America was swept up in World Cup fever, and over ninety thousand fans showed up to the Rose Bowl in Pasadena, California, for the game. It was the biggest crowd ever for a women's sporting event—the American women had broken the record again. Even before the game was played, Mia and her teammates had proved that women's sports could be successful. Now all they needed was a World Cup win to drive the point home.

The two teams were evenly matched. Each time either went on the attack, the defense collapsed and cleared the ball. Time and time again Mia raced downfield and tried to get open, but the tough Chinese defenders prevented her from scoring. The Chinese made some very physical challenges on American players. Back and forth, back and forth. No one could find an advantage.

At the end of regulation play, the game was scoreless, and in the final minutes the US team had lost Michelle Akers, who had to leave the game after taking a knock to the head. The game entered a fifteen-minute overtime period. A single score, a golden goal, would win the game for either team. Whoever scored first would be the champion.

In the first overtime, China nearly broke through on a corner, but Kristine Lilly made a goal-line header to save the game. Then another fifteen-minute period was played. Although the United States pressured the rapidly tiring Chinese, overtime passed without a goal. After 120 minutes of exhausting play, the World Cup would have to be decided on penalty kicks.

In a penalty kick situation, each team selects five players who alternate taking single shots from a fixed place twelve yards from the goal. The goalkeeper cannot move until the ball is struck. Whichever team makes the most goals out of the five attempts wins.

In soccer, it is very difficult to stop a penalty kick, simply because goalies aren't big enough to cover the entire net. To stop a shot, keepers have to anticipate where the ball is going. It's part guesswork and a lot psychology. Keepers study film of the opposition taking penalty shots to learn which direction each player likes to go in an attempt to help them during penalty kicks. Briana Scurry had done her homework, but now she'd be put to the test.

The Americans hadn't been involved in a penalty kick situation in four years. Mia didn't care to end a game that way and had even admitted that she lacked confidence in penalty kick situations. But no one was surprised when Coach DiCicco selected Mia Hamm, along with Carla Overbeck, Joy Fawcett, Kristine Lilly, and Brandi Chastain to shoot for the United States.

The Chinese shot first. Their first two players scored, as did Carla Overbeck and Joy Fawcett for the United States. Then Liu Ying stepped up to challenge Briana Scurry. Scurry guessed the Chinese woman would shoot to the right side of the goal and she dove accordingly. *Thump!* The ball ricocheted off her hands and away from the net. No goal! The score remained 2–2. Kristine Lilly then scored to put the United States ahead, but seconds later another Chinese player beat Scurry to make it 3–3.

Mia placed her ball on the spot, took a deep breath, and approached the ball as ninety thousand soccer fans cheered and millions more around the world watched on television. She knew this was the most important kick of her career.

She stood several yards behind the ball and concentrated. Then she took a few quick steps and kicked the ball with her right foot. The ball went on a line just inside the right post. The Chinese goal-keeper tried to stop it, but she couldn't. GOAL! The Americans were up 4–3. Mia ran over and jumped into the arms of her teammates.

Moments later, Chinese star Sun Wen stepped up and buried her penalty kick to tie the score. The game came down to a single kick by Brandi Chastain. If she made it, the United States would win the World Cup.

Without hesitation, Chastain placed the ball, stepped back, and drilled the ball into the side netting. The Americans had won!

The crowd roared. Pandemonium broke out as over ninety thousand fans in the Rose Bowl started screaming and yelling. In an instant Brandi was engulfed by her teammates, all elated to be world champions once again. Two of the first three Women's World Cups now belonged to the United States. All their dreams had come true and they had made their sport a success in the process, inspiring count-less young girls across the globe to get more involved in sports and athletics.

"We came to understand," Mia said later, "that this World Cup wasn't just about us winning. This is a historic event far beyond any single result. If we lose sight of that, everything we did would be for nothing." As millions of young girls playing soccer around the world could attest, Mia Hamm has never ever lost sight of what is most important. She has always been an ambassador of the sport while being its biggest star.

CHAPTER TWELVE
2000–2001

GOLDEN DREAMS

The 1999 season had been like a dream come true for the United States and women's soccer. Thanks in large part to the outstanding play of the US women's national team, women's soccer was getting more attention than ever. In response, plans were announced to start a new women's soccer league, the Women's United Soccer Association (WUSA). Games were slotted to begin in 2001.

Meanwhile, the 2000 season was shaping up to be one of the busiest Mia Hamm and her teammates had ever seen. Along with their usual schedule of games, that year would see the inauguration of a new international contest, the Women's Gold Cup, to be played in the United States. It would also find them in Australia for the 2000 Olympics, defending their 1996 gold medal.

The team started off strong, taking the Australian Cup in January. Then, in early February, they suffered the first of two consecutive losses to Norway, breaking a forty-one-game winning streak. After that, though, they roared through the next thirteen games with eleven wins, one loss, and one tie. Then, in late June and early July, came the Women's Gold Cup.

The first game was an 11–0 shutout against Trinidad and Tobago. Mia scored two goals during this match, the 119th and 120th of her career. The next game against Costa Rica was also a decisive win, with the United States blasting eight goals. Then came a nail-biter against the increasingly powerful Brazilian team. Before a near-sellout crowd in Foxborough, Massachusetts, the teams battled back and forth for a full ninety minutes, only to have the game end in a 0–0 tie. A few days later the US team faced Canada in the semifinals. Mia helped her team advance to the finals by slamming in a second-half goal in the 4–1 victory.

The finals were played in Foxborough before more than twenty thousand fans. The United States was facing strong competitor Brazil once again, in a matchup sure to be an instant classic. Brazil came on strong and shut down the United States' attacks again and again. Then, just before halftime,

Mia Hamm caught the Brazilians off guard. Usually a right-field player, she suddenly appeared with the ball near the left side of the goal. The Brazilians scrambled to mark her. But Mia didn't shoot. Instead, she crossed the ball to Tiffeny Milbrett, who had made a move toward the goal while everyone focused on Mia. The pass was perfect—Milbrett simply deflected the ball into the net for the one and only goal of the game. The United States won!

Two months later, the US team had added five more wins, one loss, and four ties to their stats. Each game helped them prepare for their biggest challenge of the year: the Olympics. That year, the US team would face stiff competition in the first round as they were grouped with China, Norway, and Nigeria.

First up was Norway. In the six games the United States had played against the Norwegians to date, they had lost three, won two, and tied one. How their first Olympic game would end was anybody's guess. Yet from the outset, the United States dominated. In the eighteenth minute, Milbrett scored a goal that many claimed was the oddest ever seen; the ball hit both posts *and* the crossbar before finally landing in the net! Mia Hamm sweetened the 1–0 lead six minutes later. The United States won that game before tying China and beating Nigeria to advance to the next round atop their group.

After four days of rest, the United States managed to eke out a 1–0 win in the semifinals against Brazil, thanks to a goal by Mia Hamm in the sixtieth minute of the game.

The Americans had fought their way to the finals. They would have to face Norway again for the gold medal.

Anyone who saw the match later agreed that it was one of the best, most intense games the United States ever played. The Americans went up early with a goal from Milbrett that was assisted by Mia. The Norwegians struck back with a pair of goals to give them a 2–1 lead late in the game. Then Mia sent a cross pass over the Norwegian captain's head to Milbrett, who headed it straight into the goal to tie it all up.

It was still tied at the end of ninety minutes, forcing the game into overtime. As the minutes ticked by, the two teams battled for a sudden-death victory. Twelve minutes later, the ball finally landed in the net—the United States' net. The goal was controversial since it had rebounded off the arm of a

Norwegian player before she booted it into the goal. But the referee allowed it. This year, the US team would have to be satisfied returning home wearing silver medals rather than gold.

The exhausted US national team played only three more games that season, ending their long year with a record of twenty-five wins, eight draws, and only six losses. For Mia Hamm, it had been a year of great triumph. She had played an astonishing 2,571 minutes in 33 games, and had added 13 goals and 16 assists.

The constant travel and playing were hard on Mia, her body, and her marriage. She and her husband both traveled often and in many ways lived separate lives. They decided that divorce was the right option. While Mia was saddened to see her marriage end, she knew that it was for the best. By this point, Mia had been on the national team for fourteen years—almost half her life—and it took up so much of her time and energy that she had very little time for herself.

She loved the game, she really did, but its demands were taking a toll.

CHAPTER THIRTEEN
2001–2003

A WORLD CHAMPION TO THE END

The Women's United Soccer Association's inaugural season began in April of 2001. The league was composed of eight teams. Sprinkled throughout those teams were players who were also members of the national team, including Mia Hamm.

Mia would play just three games with the national team in 2001. But as a midfielder and then a forward with the Washington Freedom, she played in nineteen of the twenty-one matches. She led her team with six goals and four assists. More than once in the season, she showed just how powerful a player she was, exciting the crowds with her skill, technique, and speed. In a late-April game, she turned around a one-goal deficit with an assist to tie, then scored a goal off a dead ball. Both came in the last ten minutes of the game.

Still, despite Mia's strong play, the Freedom would end their first season with a disappointing record of six wins, twelve losses, and three ties. Off the field, Mia was struggling, too. Besides her commitments to the US national team and the Freedom, she also had responsibilities to the Mia Hamm Foundation and the various companies that had signed her for endorsements.

Not long after her divorce became national news, her engagement to baseball superstar Nomar Garciaparra of the Boston Red Sox also became public. Mia had never liked being in the spotlight and all the attention bothered her. To top it all off, she was plagued by shoulder and knee injuries. The knee problem finally sidelined her in November.

When the national team began its 2002 season in January, it did so without Mia. In February, she had arthroscopic surgery on her knee. She was out when the Freedom's season started in April. But in the first week of June, the announcement came that Mia Hamm was ready to rejoin the Freedom's lineup. Mia hadn't played for seven months, the longest break in her career, and she was itching to get back on the field.

"I wanted to be back," she said. "But the whole thing was making sure I was ready."

"Pushing her too early was the worst thing we could have done for her," added the Freedom's general manager, Katy Button. "We wanted her back when she felt confident."

Confident was exactly how Mia felt when she took to the field for the second half of a game against the Boston Breakers on June 12. Within seven minutes, she had scored the game-winning goal!

The Freedom roared through the second half of their season, winning ten games in a row. In the first of those ten, Mia scored two goals; a month later, she assisted on a goal to help the Freedom beat San Diego. But it was on August 4, in a game against Atlanta, that Mia proved she was back in top form. She was simply unstoppable, first launching a corner kick to teammate Pu Wei for the first of the team's three goals. Later, she split the defense to score the second goal unassisted. Then came another corner kick to Bai Jie, who headed the ball into the net for the third, game-winning goal.

Mia ended the Freedom season with eight goals and six assists for a total of twenty-two points—all in just over five hundred minutes of play, an average of one goal every sixty-three minutes!

Mia had also rejoined the national team. She played her first game and scored her first goal in late July. In September, she scored a hat trick and contributed three assists in an 8–2 rout of Scotland. That same month, she added two more goals in a game against Russia. Her last goal came in her last game, in the Women's Gold Cup final against Canada. Four minutes into overtime with the score tied at one, Mia charged past her defender and blasted the ball over the Canadian goalkeeper's head to give her team the win.

It had been a season of highs and lows for Mia. For the first time, she had not been a regular starter for either the Freedom or the national team. The next year, however, would find her firmly back in the forefront of women's soccer players.

The WUSA knew that the 2003 season was likely to be challenging for the league. As many as fifty of their players also played for national teams around the world. These players would be called away often to compete in international matches. The biggest of these competitions was the 2003 FIFA Women's World Cup.

In the months leading up to the Cup, the Freedom played twenty-one games, of which they won nine, lost eight, and tied four, giving them fourth place overall in the league. Mia had her best season to date. She led the league in assists and tied for the lead in game-winning goals. Her greatest game came in early August, when she scored her first-ever WUSA hat trick to help the Freedom earn a berth in the Founders Cup, the WUSA's championship.

In the semifinals, against Boston, she slammed in a goal during an overtime penalty-kick shootout after 105 minutes of scoreless play. Washington won the shootout and advanced to the finals. The championship game also went into overtime and in the fifth minute, Mia looked to end the tie with a free-kick blast that hit the bar and landed in the Atlanta Beat goalkeeper's hands. Luckily, her teammate Abby Wambach managed to stick the ball in the net as the overtime minutes ticked down. It was the Freedom's first Founders Cup!

Sadly, that game would prove to be the last played by the league. Since its formation in 2001, the WUSA had been losing money and watching its fan base dwindle. In mid-September, the announcement came that the league was suspending play until further notice. Although they hoped to put together a series of exhibition games, there would be no true season in 2004.

Mia was disappointed the WUSA was not a success, but she knew she needed to put her feelings aside and concentrate on the next big match—the World Cup that was to begin in one week.

CHAPTER FOURTEEN
2003–2004

GOLDEN AGAIN

"There is no doubt this Women's World Cup will be different from the last tournament," Mia said shortly before the competition. "Women's [soccer] has made so many strides since 1999. We have new faces, new personalities.... The future of the women's game is definitely bright."

The Women's World Cup was originally scheduled to be played in China in 2003. But that fall, a new and deadly disease called SARS was plaguing the region. Health professionals worldwide cautioned people not to travel to the area unless absolutely necessary. So the United States stepped forward and offered to host the games instead. The infrastructure from the last World Cup was still in place and they had already hosted the event. It would be easiest for the United States to put on a tournament of that size and caliber in little to no time.

Going into the World Cup, the US national team had a record of eleven wins, one loss, and three draws. Nine of those wins were shutouts, four of which were won by margins of five or more goals. The team looked strong and as defending World Cup champions, they were eager to come out on top again.

The first game was against the tough Swedish team. Their defense gave the United States a run for their money, but in the end, Mia made a huge impact. On three different occasions, she was able to create space and cross the ball to teammates who put it where it counted—in the net. Mia's expert passing gave the United States a 3–1 victory and the chance to face Nigeria.

Once again, Mia made the difference in the team's 5–0 win. She scored on a penalty shot in the sixth minute of the game, blasted in another unassisted goal in the twelfth minute, and assisted on a third goal two minutes into the second half. She came close to scoring a hat trick, but twice the goalkeeper managed to get just a fingertip on her shots.

Mia sat out the third game, a 3–0 victory over North Korea, and came back fully rested for a difficult game against Norway. It was a classic nail-biter between the two champion-caliber teams. In the end, the United States managed to win 1–0 to advance to the semifinals against Germany.

Unfortunately, that would be as far as they would advance in the tournament. Germany shut them out 3–0. The United States would play just one other game in the tournament, to determine which team would place third in the World Cup. The United States beat Canada 3–1 in that match, where the US team scored their one thousandth goal. Shannon Boxx scored the historic goal and Mia got the assist.

The US team played two more matches to end its season with an impressive 17 wins, 2 losses, and 4 ties. Mia had played 17 of those games, starting in 15, and chalked up 8 goals and 9 assists. She had spent 1,353 minutes on the field with the national team on top of the time played with the Freedom. Off the field, she married Nomar Garciaparra on November 22 in a beautiful ceremony.

With the WUSA still in flux, Mia focused almost completely on the US national team during the 2004 season. Her eyes were on her next major goal—a medal at the 2004 Olympics in Athens, Greece. Since the US team had only brought home a silver medal in the last Olympics, the team had to go through the qualifying rounds in order to be assured a spot in the Games. Mia chipped in right off the bat, scoring two goals in the February qualifier against Trinidad and Tobago. By the time the Olympics opened in mid-August, she had added five more goals to her stat sheet, including the 150th of her career.

Before the Olympics, Mia had announced that it would be her last international tournament. The Athens Olympics would be her swan song, her goodbye to a sport she had loved for her entire life.

The first match of the Olympics was against the host nation of Greece. To the Greek crowd's disappointment, the United States won 3–0, with Mia scoring the third goal early in the second half. Three days later, in a match against Brazil, Mia scored again, this time on a clutch penalty kick in the fifty-eighth minute of play. The United States tied in their third contest, against Australia, but bested Japan and Germany to advance to the gold-medal game of the competition and a matchup against Brazil and their new phenom, Marta.

The game was an intense end-to-end battle as the two best teams in the world fought to prove that they were worthy of being number one. Going into that game, Brazil had held their opponents scoreless for 283 minutes. The United States would have to break through that strong defense. It was an emotional night. Mia was playing in what would amount to her last meaningful game in a US jersey, and as a tribute she was given the captain's armband.

Time and again, Brazil launched rockets at the US keeper that would have been goals if not for the play of Briana Scurry and some lucky narrow misses. The Brazilians were so technically gifted it was frightening. Left fullback Rosana's composure on the ball was outstanding. In the first five minutes, she dribbled out a double team with a series of moves that embarrassed two American players.

In the thirty-ninth minute, veteran Brandi Chastain cut off a pass at the center circle. Brandi's touch was heavy and it fell between her and the Brazilian Formiga. The two met at the ball at the same time, and the ball popped up and struck Brandi's arm. Brandi came away with the ball and played it to Lindsay Tarpley. Tarpley, only a junior at the University of North Carolina, dribbled to goal as the Brazilian defense backpedaled, giving Tarpley tons of room. She took two more touches and then ripped a laser into the left-side netting. The young

American put the United States on the scoreboard with an emphatic goal.

The score remained 1–0 for another thirty-four minutes. The US team had almost scored again: Mia had put Abby Wambach into the corner, where she shed her defender and crossed the ball to the back post, where Kristine Lilly got a knee on it, but Brazilian keeper Andréia made a great save. Mia had almost scored her fourth goal in four games.

Then Cristiane, who had come off the bench the last time these two teams met, put on a show. The Americans gave the ball away on a miscommunication during a throw-in. Formiga ended up with the ball and immediately noticed Joy Fawcett pushing ahead of Cristiane. Formiga hit a beautiful long ball that dropped eight yards from the left corner of the penalty box. Joy Fawcett missed the slide tackle. Cristiane rode the challenge and blew by both American defenders. As Cristiane got into the box, three defenders collapsed on her. She slid the ball toward the end line, stopped it, faked right, and took one touch toward goal. She had created only an inch of space, but it was enough to send in a hard and low cross across the face of the goal. Briana came off her line to palm the ball away, but it fell right to Brazilian player Pretinha, who tapped it in. And with the smallest of moves, Pretinha had tied the gold-medal game in the seventy-third minute.

The match stayed tied through regulation, despite the fact that the Brazilians were all over the American backline from their goal until the ninetieth minute. Briana had to weather a number of close calls, including a shot that hit the left post. The two teams went into one fifteen-minute overtime, then another. In the 112th minute of the exhausting and brutally physical game, in which there were twenty-eight fouls called, the United States made their last push. After pumping a long ball into the box from midfield, the United States won a corner. Kristine Lilly took the corner and hit a sublime ball to the back post, where Abby Wambach was able to head the ball on goal. The Brazilian captain tried to head it off the line, but instead the ball shot up and into the goal. Wambach was credited with the goal, and the American women were gold medalists once again. Mia was able to end her career the same way she started it: as a world champion.

After the game, Mia was asked about what she thought her legacy would be. She answered by talking about her team.

"This team right here," she said. "This team that never gave up. And every single player made a difference. Nomar, we have one for the family. I love you. I love this team. Unbelievable."

For Mia Hamm, this sweet victory marked the end of a remarkable career. She wanted to have

Shaun Botterill / staff / Getty Images

JOY FAWCETT AND MIA HAMM EMBRACE ON THE MEDAL PODIUM.

more time to spend with her husband, and they were thinking of starting a family. She also wanted to dedicate herself more fully to her charitable foundation. And she knew that she was leaving the team in good hands: Abby Wambach, Shannon Boxx, and Heather O'Reilly had won gold with her, and they would help usher in a new era of excellence for US women's soccer. Still, Mia knew some people thought she was crazy. After all, she was at the top of her game.

Even though she still had the ability to play, Mia had begun to look forward to new challenges and was happy to go out on her own terms. When she first saw a soccer ball, there wasn't an opportunity to play soccer in the Olympics as a woman, nor was there a women's World Cup. Back then she could have never imagined playing in games of this caliber or being able to play professionally. But she had and she did, and she changed the nature of the game on and off the field with her play, because she was just that good. She had been the youngest player to ever play for the national team in 1987 at just 15 years, 140 days old. She had had twenty-eight games in which she scored two goals and had scored a goal in twenty-six states. When she scored at least one goal, the US women's national team had a record of 97–3–4. She had played in three World Cups and two Olympics. She had two Olympic gold medals, an Olympic silver medal, and two World Cup championships. She held the record for most goals by a female soccer player in international competitions, which stood for ten years until Abby Wambach bested her total in 2013. In Mia's mind, she had done all she could playing soccer.

"Will I miss playing soccer?" she mused. "Absolutely. But I'm at peace with my decision. It definitely is time to move on with my life. I've had my time. It's someone else's turn."

But before she was allowed to hang up her cleats, there was one other task she had to perform. She was asked by her fellow US Olympians to carry the American flag in the closing ceremonies. It was the first time a soccer player, male or female, had been asked.

"I am truly speechless," Mia said. "I was expecting to be a follower tomorrow night, just to go wherever I was pointed. Now I am carrying the flag. It is a tremendous honor. Leading my country and the US Olympic team, which I am so proud to be a part of, is something truly special."

"Truly special" is how a generation of soccer fans would undoubtedly classify Mia Hamm. Through her determination, good sportsmanship, and genuine love of the game, she has inspired countless future players while bringing women's soccer to the forefront of American sports.

CHAPTER FIFTEEN
2004–PRESENT

LIFE GOES ON

Mia Hamm officially retired on December 8, 2004. She left the US team in great shape, and their success continued with the help of the goal-scoring machine Abby Wambach. Meanwhile, Mia and her husband started their own team when Mia gave birth to twin daughters, Ava and Grace, in 2007, and a son, Garrett, in 2012.

"I've achieved many wonderful goals, but my family is what I'm most proud of," Mia said. "Having a happy, healthy family is everything."

Mia's soccer legacy remains strong. She is one of the most popular sports figures in the world—even today! Though she no longer plays soccer, she is still very busy. Mia continues her charity work through the Mia Hamm Foundation, Athletes for Hope, and other organizations dedicated to doing good. She also gives back to the community and raises money for good causes by putting on charity soccer events in Southern California. She even wrote a children's book a few years after her retirement. At one point, she was the inspiration for the logo of a now-defunct women's pro league.

In November 2013, Mia Hamm was the first woman ever inducted into the FIFA-approved World Football Hall of Fame. Mia continues to be a major influence in the sport in everything she does. Twice in one week in late 2014, Mia made international headlines again. First, she was named to the board of directors of AS Roma, a professional Italian football club based in Rome. The Roma connection brought her back to her time living in Italy, when she first fell in love with the sport of soccer. Then she was part of the winning bid of the next Los Angeles–based Major League Soccer team, which will join the MLS in 2017. She also hopes to help the Los Angeles Football Club start a women's team when the time is right.

Mia once said, "If I had to give up what I'm doing, I wouldn't be happy."

On the field and off, Mia has brought enthusiasm and her best effort to her every move. Today, Mia's most important role remains as an ambassador for her sport and for female athletes in general.

"I've experienced every emotion on the field," she once confided to a reporter, "sadness, fear, and happiness. [Soccer] made me who I am. I was given a tremendous gift and believe I was given it for a reason."

For millions of her fans, the reason has been the opportunity to watch her play. The gift she gives back is the proof that soccer is a game for everyone.

TURN THE PAGE FOR MORE FUN FACTS!

MIA HAMM

MIA'S CAREER HIGHLIGHTS

1987:

 Youngest woman (at age 15) ever to play with
 the US national team

1991:

 Member of the Women's World Cup
 US championship team
 Youngest player (at age 19) on the Women's
 World Cup championship team

1993:

 Completed University of North Carolina career
 as ACC's all-time leading scorer in goals (103),
 assists (72), and points (278)
 Leading scorer (with 6 goals) of silver medal–
 winning US team at the World University
 Games

1994:

 Named US Soccer's Female Athlete of the Year
 Had her UNC number (19) retired

1995:

Named US Soccer's Female Athlete of the Year

Member of the Women's World Cup third place
US national team

Named US Women's Cup MVP

1996:

Named US Soccer's Female Athlete of the Year

Member of the gold medal–winning US Olympic
team

1997:

Named US Soccer's Female Athlete of the Year

Named US Women's Cup MVP

Named Women's Sports Foundation Team Athlete of
the Year

Named to *People* magazine's "50 Most Beautiful
People" list

1998:

Named US Soccer's Female Athlete of the Year

Won ESPN's "Espy" Award for Female Athlete of the
Year

Amateur Athletic Foundation World Trophy recipient

Member of the gold medal–winning team at the
Goodwill Games in New York City

First US player to score 100 goals in his or her career

1999:

Became the world's leading goal scorer in
   international competition, male or female
Formed the Mia Hamm Foundation
Member of the Women's World Cup
   US championship team
Won ESPN's "Espy" Award for Female Athlete of
   the Year and Soccer Player of the Year

2000:

Member of the silver medal–winning US Olympic
   team

2001:

Founding member of the Women's United Soccer
   Association
Began career in WUSA with the Washington
   Freedom and led all Freedom scorers in goals
   and assists
Named FIFA Women's World Player of the Year

2002:

Named FIFA Women's World Player of the Year
Led Freedom to Founders Cup championship game

2003:

Best season in the WUSA: led the WUSA in assists (11) and tied for the league lead in game-winning goals (4)

Assisted in Washington Freedom's success as Founders Cup champions

Graced the cover of *Sports Illustrated* in September; only the second female soccer player to appear on the cover

Member of the Women's World Cup third place US national team

2004:

Member of the gold medal–winning US Olympic team

Held record as world's all-time leading scorer, male or female, with 158 goals scored in international competition (broken by Abby Wambach in 2013)

MIA'S GOALS AND ASSISTS

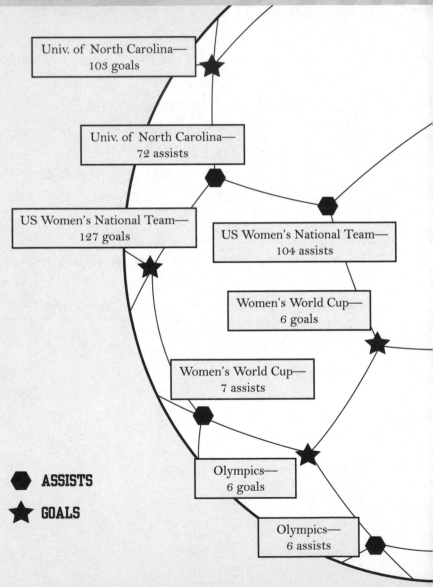

Univ. of North Carolina—
103 goals

Univ. of North Carolina—
72 assists

US Women's National Team—
127 goals

US Women's National Team—
104 assists

Women's World Cup—
6 goals

Women's World Cup—
7 assists

Olympics—
6 goals

Olympics—
6 assists

ASSISTS

GOALS

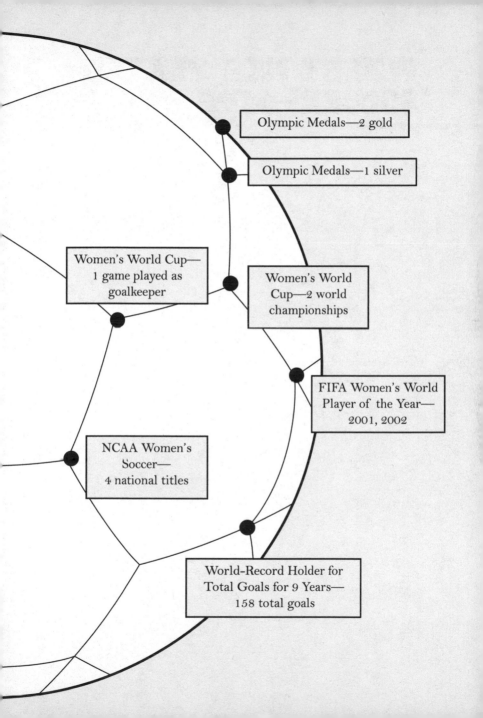

Olympic Medals—2 gold

Olympic Medals—1 silver

Women's World Cup—
1 game played as
goalkeeper

Women's World
Cup—2 world
championships

FIFA Women's World
Player of the Year—
2001, 2002

NCAA Women's
Soccer—
4 national titles

World-Record Holder for
Total Goals for 9 Years—
158 total goals

WHERE MIA PLAYED SOCCER—MAP

SEE NEXT PAGE FOR A LIST OF LOCATIONS.

WHERE MIA PLAYED SOCCER—LOCATIONS

RALEIGH, NORTH CAROLINA
(North Carolina
State University)
1 game, 1989 NCAA
Championship

**CHAPEL HILL,
NORTH CAROLINA**
(University of
North Carolina)
1 game, 1990 NCAA
Championship

PANYU, CHINA
2 games, 1991 Women's
World Cup

FOSHAN, CHINA
2 games, 1991 Women's
World Cup

GUANGZHOU, CHINA
2 games, 1991 Women's
World Cup

**CHAPEL HILL,
NORTH CAROLINA**
(University of
North Carolina)
1 game, 1992 NCAA
Championship

**CHAPEL HILL,
NORTH CAROLINA**
(University of
North Carolina)
1 game, 1993 NCAA
Championship

GÄVLE, SWEDEN
4 games, 1995 Women's
World Cup

HELSINGBORG, SWEDEN
1 game, 1995 Women's
World Cup

VÄSTERÅS, SWEDEN
1 game, 1995 Women's
World Cup

ORLANDO, FLORIDA
2 games, 1996 Olympics

ATHENS, GEORGIA
2 games, 1996 Olympics

**EAST RUTHERFORD,
NEW JERSEY**
1 game, 1999 Women's
World Cup

CHICAGO, ILLINOIS
1 game, 1999 Women's World Cup

BOSTON, MASSACHUSETTS
1 game, 1999 Women's World Cup

WASHINGTON, DC
1 game, 1999 Women's World Cup

SAN FRANCISCO, CALIFORNIA
1 game, 1999 Women's World Cup

LOS ANGELES, CALIFORNIA
1 game, 1999 Women's World Cup

MELBOURNE, AUSTRALIA
3 games, 2000 Olympics

CANBERRA, AUSTRALIA
1 game, 2000 Olympics

SYDNEY, AUSTRALIA
1 game, 2000 Olympics

WASHINGTON, DC
1 game, 2003 Women's World Cup

PHILADELPHIA, PENNSYLVANIA
1 game, 2003 Women's World Cup

FOXBOROUGH, MASSACHUSETTS
1 game, 2003 Women's World Cup

PORTLAND, OREGON
1 game, 2003 Women's World Cup

CARSON, CALIFORNIA
1 game, 2003 Women's World Cup

HERAKLION, GREECE
2 games, 2004 Olympics

THESSALONIKI, GREECE
3 games, 2004 Olympics

PIRAEUS, GREECE
1 game, 2004 Olympics

MIA'S STATS

COLLEGE STATS

Year	Games Played	Games Started	Goals	Assists	Points
1989	23	18	21	4	46
1990	22	22	24	19	67
1992	25	21	32	33	97
1993	22	22	26	16	68
TOTALS	92	83	103	72	278

WUSA STATS

Year	Games Played	Games Started	Goals	Assists	Points
2001	19	19	6	4	16
2002	11	1	8	6	22
2003	19	16	11	11	33
TOTALS	49	36	25	21	71

OLYMPIC STATS

Year	Games Played	Games Started	Goals	Assists	Points
1996	4	4	1	3	5
2000	5	5	2	2	6
2004	5	5	2	2	6
TOTALS	14	14	5	7	17

NATIONAL TEAM STATS

Year	Games Played	Games Started	Goals	Assists	Points
1987	7	4	0	0	0
1988	8	7	0	0	0
1989	1	0	0	0	0
1990	5	1	4	1	9
1991	28	24	10	4	24
1992	2	2	1	0	2
1993	16	16	10	4	24
1994	9	9	10	5	25
1995	21	20	19	18	56
1996	23	23	9	18	36
1997	16	16	18	6	42
1998	21	21	20	20	60
1999	26	26	13	16	42
2000	33	29	13	14	40
2001	3	2	2	2	6
2002	9	6	7	5	19
2003	17	15	8	9	25
2004	29	27	14	20	48
TOTALS	**274**	**248**	**158**	**142**	**458**